THE PELICAN SHAKESPEARE
GENERAL EDITORS

STEPHEN ORGEL
A. R. BRAUNMULLER

Macbeth

Ellen Terry as Lady Macbeth, 1888

William Shakespeare

———

Macbeth

EDITED BY STEPHEN ORGEL

PENGUIN BOOKS·

PENGUIN BOOKS

Published by the Penguin Group

Penguin Group (USA) Inc., 375 Hudson Street, New York, New York 10014, U.S.A.

Penguin Books Ltd, 80 Strand, London WC2R 0RL, England

Penguin Books Australia Ltd, 250 Camberwell Road, Camberwell, Victoria 3124, Australia

Penguin Books Canada Ltd, 10 Alcorn Avenue, Toronto, Ontario, Canada M4V 3B2

Penguin Books India (P) Ltd, 11 Community Centre, Panchsheel Park, New Delhi – 110 017, India

Penguin Books (N.Z.) Ltd, Cnr Rosedale and Airborne Roads, Albany, Auckland, New Zealand

Penguin Books (South Africa) (Pty) Ltd, 24 Sturdee Avenue,
Rosebank, Johannesburg 2196, South Africa

Penguin Books Ltd, Registered Offices: 80 Strand, London WC2R 0RL, England

Macbeth edited by Alfred Harbage published in the
United States of America in Penguin Books 1956
Revised edition published 1971
This new edition edited by Stephen Orgel published 2000

10

Copyright © Penguin Books Inc., 1956, 1971
Copyright © Penguin Putnam Inc., 2000
All rights reserved

ISBN 0-14-07.1478-2

Printed in the United States of America
Set in Garamond
Designed by Virginia Norey

Contents

Publisher's Note

IT IS ALMOST half a century since the first volumes of the
Pelican Shakespeare appeared under the general editorship
of Alfred Harbage. The fact that a new edition, rather
than simply a revision, has been undertaken reflects the
profound changes textual and critical studies of Shakespeare have undergone in the past twenty years. For the
new Pelican series, the texts of the plays and poems have
been thoroughly revised in accordance with recent schol-
arship, and in some cases have been entirely reedited. New
introductions and notes have been provided in all the volumes. But the new Shakespeare is also designed as a successor to the original series; the previous editions have
been taken into account, and the advice of the previous
editors has been solicited where it was feasible to do so.

Certain textual features of the new Pelican Shakespeare
should be particularly noted. All lines are numbered that
contain a word, phrase, or allusion explained in the
glossarial notes. In addition, for convenience, every tenth
line is also numbered, in italics when no annotation is indicated. The intrusive and often inaccurate place headings
inserted by early editors are omitted (as is becoming standard practice), but for the convenience of those who miss
them, an indication of locale now appears as the first item
in the annotation of each scene.

In the interest of both elegance and utility, each speech
prefix is set in a separate line when the speaker's lines are
in verse, except when those words form the second half of
a verse line. Thus the verse form of the speech is kept vi-
sually intact. What is printed as verse and what is printed
as prose has, in general, the authority of the original texts.
Departures from the original texts in this regard have only
the authority of editorial tradition and the judgment of
the Pelican editors; and, in a few instances, are admittedly
arbitrary.

The Theatrical World

ECONOMIC REALITIES determined the theatrical world in which Shakespeare's plays were written, performed, and received. For centuries in England, the primary theatrical tradition was nonprofessional. Craft guilds (or "mysteries") provided religious drama – mystery plays – as part of the celebration of religious and civic festivals, and schools and universities staged classical and neoclassical drama in both Latin and English as part of their curricula. In these forms, drama was established and socially acceptable. Professional theater, in contrast, existed on the margins of society. The acting companies were itinerant; playhouses could be any available space – the great halls of the aristocracy, town squares, civic halls, inn yards, fair booths, or open fields – and income was sporadic, dependent on the passing of the hat or on the bounty of local patrons. The actors, moreover, were considered little better than vagabonds, constantly in danger of arrest or expulsion.

In the late 1560s and 1570s, however, English professional theater began to gain respectability. Wealthy aristocrats fond of drama – the Lord Admiral, for example, or the Lord Chamberlain – took acting companies under their protection so that the players technically became members of their households and were no longer subject to arrest as homeless or masterless men. Permanent theaters were first built at this time as well, allowing the companies to control and charge for entry to their performances.

Shakespeare's livelihood, and the stunning artistic explosion in which he participated, depended on pragmatic and architectural effort. Professional theater requires ways to restrict access to its offerings; if it does not, and admission fees cannot be charged, the actors do not get paid, the costumes go to a pawnbroker, and there is no such thing as a professional, ongoing theatrical tradition. The answer to that economic need arrived in the late 1560s and 1570s with the creation of the so-called public or amphitheater playhouse. Recent discoveries indicate that the precursor of the Globe playhouse in London (where Shakespeare's mature plays were presented) and the Rose theater (which presented Christopher Marlowe's plays and some of Shakespeare's earliest ones) was the Red Lion theater of 1567. Archaeological studies of the foundations of the Rose and Globe theaters have revealed that the open-air theater of the 1590s and later was probably a polygonal building with fourteen to twenty or twenty-four sides, multistoried, from 75 to 100 feet in diameter, with a raised, partly covered "thrust" stage that projected into a group of standing patrons, or "groundlings," and a covered gallery, seating up to 2,500 or more (very crowded) spectators.

These theaters might have been about half full on any given day, though the audiences were larger on holidays or when a play was advertised, as old and new were, through printed playbills posted around London. The metropolitan area's late-Tudor, early-Stuart population (circa 1590-1620) has been estimated at about 150,000 to 250,000. It has been supposed that in the mid-1590s there were about 15,000 spectators per week at the public theaters; thus, as many as 10 percent of the local population went to the theater regularly. Consequently, the theaters' repertories – the plays available for this experienced and frequent audience – had to change often: in the month between September 15 and October 15, 1595, for instance, the Lord Admiral's Men performed twenty-eight times in eighteen different plays.

Since natural light illuminated the amphitheaters' stages, performances began between noon and two o'clock and ran without a break for two or three hours. They often concluded with a jig, a fencing display, or some other nondramatic exhibition. Weather conditions determined the season for the amphitheaters: plays were performed every day (including Sundays, sometimes, to clerical dismay) except during Lent – the forty days before Easter – or periods of plague, or sometimes during the summer months when law courts were not in session and the most affluent members of the audience were not in London.

To a modern theatergoer, an amphitheater stage like that of the Rose or Globe would appear an unfamiliar mixture of plainness and elaborate decoration. Much of the structure was carved or painted, sometimes to imitate marble; elsewhere, as under the canopy projecting over the stage, to represent the stars and the zodiac. Appropriate painted canvas pictures (of Jerusalem, for example, if the play was set in that city) were apparently hung on the wall behind the acting area, and tragedies were accompanied by black hangings, presumably something like crepe festoons or bunting. Although these theaters did not employ what we would call scenery, early modern spectators saw numerous large props, such as the "bar" at which a prisoner stood during a trial, the "mossy bank" where lovers reclined, an arbor for amorous conversation, a chariot, gallows, tables, trees, beds, thrones, writing desks, and so forth. Audiences might learn a scene's location from a sign (reading "Athens," for example) carried across the stage (as in Bertolt Brecht's twentieth-century productions). Equally captivating (and equally irritating to the theater's enemies) were the rich costumes and personal props the actors used: the most valuable items in the surviving theatrical inventories are the swords, gowns, robes, crowns, and other items worn or carried by the performers.

Magic appealed to Shakespeare's audiences as much as it does to us today, and the theater exploited many deceptive and spectacular devices. A winch in the loft above the stage, called "the heavens," could lower and raise actors playing gods, goddesses, and other supernatural figures to and from the main acting area, just as one or more trapdoors permitted entrances and exits to and from the area, called "hell," beneath the stage. Actors wore elementary makeup such as wigs, false beards, and face paint, and they employed pig's bladders filled with animal blood to make wounds seem more real. They had rudimentary but effective ways of pretending to behead or hang a person. Supernumeraries (stagehands or actors not needed in a particular scene) could make thunder sounds (by shaking a metal sheet or rolling an iron ball down a chute) and show lightning (by blowing inflammable resin through tubes into a flame). Elaborate fireworks enhanced the effects of dragons flying through the air or imitated such celestial phenomena as comets, shooting stars, and multiple suns. Horses' hoofbeats, bells (located perhaps in the tower above the stage), trumpets and drums, clocks, cannon shots and gunshots, and the like were common sound effects. And the music of viols, cornets, oboes, and recorders was a regular feature of theatrical performances.

For two relatively brief spans, from the late 1570s to 1590 and from 1599 to 1614, the amphitheaters competed with the so-called private, or indoor, theaters, which originated as, or later represented themselves as, educational institutions training boys as singers for church services and court performances. These indoor theaters had two features that were distinct from the amphitheaters': their personnel and their playing spaces. The amphitheaters' adult companies included both adult men, who played the male roles, and boys, who played the female roles; the private, or indoor, theater companies, on the other hand, were entirely composed of boys aged about 8 to 16, who were, or could pretend to be, candidates for singers in a church or a royal boys' choir. (Until 1660, professional theatrical companies included no women.) The playing space would appear much more familiar to modern audiences than the long-vanished amphitheaters; the later indoor theaters were, in fact, the ancestors of the typical modern theater. They were enclosed spaces, usually rectangular, with the stage filling one end of the rectangle and the audience arrayed in seats or benches across (and sometimes lining) the building's longer axis. These spaces staged plays less frequently than the public theaters (perhaps only once a week) and held far fewer spectators than the amphitheaters: about 200 to 600, as opposed to 2,500 or more. Fewer patrons mean a smaller gross income, unless each pays more. Not surprisingly, then, private theaters charged higher prices than the amphitheaters, probably sixpence, as opposed to a penny for the cheapest entry.

Protected from the weather, the indoor theaters presented plays later in the day than the amphitheaters, and used artificial illumination – candles in sconces or candelabra. But candles melt, and need replacing, snuffing, and trimming, and these practical requirements may have been part of the reason the indoor theaters introduced breaks in the performance, the intermission so dear to the heart of theatergoers and to the pocketbooks of theater concessionaires ever since. Whether motivated by the need to tend to the candles or by the entrepreneurs' wishing to sell oranges and liquor, or both, the indoor theaters eventually established the modern convention of the non-continuous performance. In the early modern "private" theater, musical performances apparently filled the intermissions, which in Stuart theater jargon seem to have been called "acts."

At the end of the first decade of the seventeenth century, the distinction between public amphitheaters and private indoor companies ceased. For various cultural, political, and economic reasons, individual companies gained control of both the public, open-air theaters and the indoor ones, and companies mixing adult men and boys took over the formerly "private" theaters. Despite the death of the boys' companies and of their highly innovative theaters (for which such luminous playwrights as Ben Jonson, George Chapman, and John Marston wrote), their playing spaces and conventions had an immense impact on subsequent plays: not merely for the intervals (which stressed the artistic and architectonic importance of "acts"), but also because they introduced political and social satire as a popular dramatic ingredient, even in tragedy, and a wider range of actorly effects, encouraged by their more intimate playing spaces.

Even the briefest sketch of the Shakespearean theatrical world would be incomplete without some comment on the social and cultural dimensions of theaters and playing in the period. In an intensely hierarchical and status-conscious society, professional actors and their ventures had hardly any respectability; as we have indicated, to protect themselves against laws designed to curb vagabondage and the increase of masterless men, actors resorted to the near-fiction that they were the servants of noble masters, and wore their distinctive livery. Hence the company for which Shakespeare wrote in the 1590s called itself the Lord Chamberlain's Men and pretended that the public, money-getting performances were in fact rehearsals for private performances before that high court official. From 1598, the Privy Council had licensed theatrical companies, and after 1603, with the accession of King James I, the companies gained explicit royal protection, just as the Queen's Men had for a time under Queen Elizabeth. The Chamberlain's Men became the King's Men, and the other companies were patronized by the other members of the royal family.

These designations were legal fictions that half-concealed an important economic and social development, the evolution away from the theater's organization on the model of the guild, a self-regulating confraternity of individual artisans, into a proto-capitalist organization. Shakespeare's company became a joint-stock company, where persons who supplied capital and, in some cases, such as Shakespeare's, capital and talent, employed themselves and others in earning a return on that capital. This development meant that actors and theater companies were outside both the traditional guild structures, which required some form of civic or royal charter, and the feudal household organization of master-and-servant. This anomalous, maverick social and economic condition made theater companies practically unruly and potentially even dangerous; consequently, numerous official bodies – including the London metropolitan and ecclesiastical authorities as well as, occasionally, the royal court itself – tried, without much success, to control and even to disband them.

Public officials had good reason to want to close the theaters: they were attractive nuisances – they drew often riotous crowds, they were always noisy, and they could be politically offensive and socially insubordinate. Until the Civil War, however, anti-theatrical forces failed to shut down professional theater, for many reasons – limited surveillance and few police powers, tensions or outright hostilities among the agencies that sought to check or channel theatrical activity, and lack of clear policies for control. Another reason must have been the theaters' undeniable popularity. Curtailing any activity enjoyed by such a substantial percentage of the population was difficult, as various Roman emperors attempting to limit circuses had learned, and the Tudor-Stuart audience was not merely large, it was socially diverse and included women. The prevalence of public entertainment in this period has been underestimated. In fact, fairs, holidays, games, sporting events, the equivalent of modern parades, freak shows, and street exhibitions all abounded, but the theater was the most widely and frequently available entertainment to which people of every class had access. That fact helps account both for its quantity and for the fear and anger it aroused.

WILLIAM SHAKESPEARE OF
STRATFORD-UPON-AVON, GENTLEMAN

Many people have said that we know very little about
William Shakespeare's life – pinheads and postcards are
often mentioned as appropriately tiny surfaces on which
to record the available information. More imaginatively
and perhaps more correctly, Ralph Waldo Emerson wrote,
"Shakespeare is the only biographer of Shakespeare. . . .
So far from Shakespeare's being the least known, he is the
one person in all modern history fully known to us."

In fact, we know more about Shakespeare's life than we
do about almost any other English writer's of his era. His
last will and testament (dated March 25, 1616) survives,
as do numerous legal contracts and court documents in-
volving Shakespeare as principal or witness, and parish
records in Stratford and London. Shakespeare appears
quite often in official records of King James's royal court,
and of course Shakespeare's name appears on numerous
title pages and in the written and recorded words of his
literary contemporaries Robert Greene, Henry Chettle,
Francis Meres, John Davies of Hereford, Ben Jonson, and
many others. Indeed, if we make due allowance for the
bloating of modern, run-of-the-mill bureaucratic records,
more information has survived over the past four hundred
years about William Shakespeare of Stratford-upon-Avon,
Warwickshire, than is likely to survive in the next four
hundred years about any reader of these words.

What we do not have are entire categories of information – Shakespeare's private letters or diaries, drafts and
revisions of poems and plays, critical prefaces or essays,
commendatory verse for other writers' works, or instructions guiding his fellow actors in their performances, for
instance – that we imagine would help us understand and
appreciate his surviving writings. For all we know, many
such data never existed as written records. Many literary

and theatrical critics, not knowing what might once have existed, more or less cheerfully accept the situation; some even make a theoretical virtue of it by claiming that such data are irrelevant to understanding and interpreting the plays and poems.

So, what do we know about William Shakespeare, the man responsible for thirty-seven or perhaps more plays, more than 150 sonnets, two lengthy narrative poems, and some shorter poems?

While many families by the name of Shakespeare (or some variant spelling) can be identified in the English Midlands as far back as the twelfth century, it seems likely that the dramatist's grandfather, Richard, moved to Snitterfield, a town not far from Stratford-upon-Avon, sometime before 1529. In Snitterfield, Richard Shakespeare leased farmland from the very wealthy Robert Arden. By 1552, Richard's son John had moved to a large house on Henley Street in Stratford-upon-Avon, the house that stands today as "The Birthplace." In Stratford, John Shakespeare traded as a glover, dealt in wool, and lent money at interest; he also served in a variety of civic posts, including "High Bailiff," the municipality's equivalent of mayor. In 1557, he married Robert Arden's youngest daughter, Mary. Mary and John had four sons – William was the oldest – and four daughters, of whom only Joan outlived her most celebrated sibling. William was baptized (an event entered in the Stratford parish church records) on April 26, 1564, and it has become customary, without any good factual support, to suppose he was born on April 23, which happens to be the feast day of Saint George, patron saint of England, and is also the date on which he died, in 1616. Shakespeare married Anne Hathaway in 1582, when he was eighteen and she was twenty-six; their first child was born five months later. It has been generally assumed that the marriage was enforced and subsequently unhappy, but these are only assumptions; it has been estimated, for instance, that up to one third of Elizabethan brides were pregnant when they married. Anne and William Shakespeare had three children: Susanna, who married a prominent local physician, John Hall; and the twins Hamnet, who died young in 1596, and Judith, who married Thomas Quiney – apparently a rather shady individual. The name Hamnet was unusual but not unique: he and his twin sister were named for their godparents, Shakespeare's neighbors Hamnet and Judith Sadler. Shakespeare's father died in 1601 (the year of *Hamlet*), and Mary Arden Shakespeare died in 1608 (the year of *Coriolanus*). William Shakespeare's last surviving direct descendant was his granddaughter Elizabeth Hall, who died in 1670.

Between the birth of the twins in 1585 and a clear reference to Shakespeare as a practicing London dramatist in Robert Greene's sensationalizing, satiric pamphlet, *Greene's Groatsworth of Wit* (1592), there is no record of where William Shakespeare was or what he was doing. These seven so-called lost years have been imaginatively filled by scholars and other students of Shakespeare: some think he traveled to Italy, or fought in the Low Countries, or studied law or medicine, or worked as an apprentice actor/writer, and so on to even more fanciful possibilities. Whatever the biographical facts for those "lost" years, Greene's nasty remarks in 1592 testify to professional envy and to the fact that Shakespeare already had a successful career in London. Speaking to his fellow playwrights, Greene warns both generally and specifically:

> . . . trust them [actors] not: for there is an upstart crow, beautified with our feathers, that with his tiger's heart wrapped in a player's hide supposes he is as well able to bombast out a blank verse as the best of you; and being an absolute Johannes Factotum, is in his own conceit the only Shake-scene in a country.

The passage mimics a line from *3 Henry VI* (hence the play must have been performed before Greene wrote) and seems to say that "Shake-scene" is both actor and playwright, a jack-of-all-trades. That same year, Henry Chettle protested Greene's remarks in *Kind-Heart's Dream,* and each of the next two years saw the publication of poems – *Venus and Adonis* and *The Rape of Lucrece,* respectively – publicly ascribed to (and dedicated by) Shakespeare. Early in 1595 he was named one of the senior members of a prominent acting company, the Lord Chamberlain's Men, when they received payment for court performances during the 1594 Christmas season.

Clearly, Shakespeare had achieved both success and reputation in London. In 1596, upon Shakespeare's application, the College of Arms granted his father the now-familiar coat of arms he had taken the first steps to obtain almost twenty years before, and in 1598, John's son – now permitted to call himself "gentleman" – took a 10 percent share in the new Globe playhouse. In 1597, he bought a substantial bourgeois house, called New Place, in Stratford – the garden remains, but Shakespeare's house, several times rebuilt, was torn down in 1759 – and over the next few years Shakespeare spent large sums buying land and making other investments in the town and its environs. Though he worked in London, his family remained in Stratford, and he seems always to have considered Stratford the home he would eventually return to. Something approaching a disinterested appreciation of Shakespeare's popular and professional status appears in Francis Meres's *Palladis Tamia* (1598), a not especially imaginative and perhaps therefore persuasive record of literary reputations. Reviewing contemporary English writers, Meres lists the titles of many of Shakespeare's plays, including one not now known, *Love's Labor's Won,* and praises his "mellifluous & hony-tongued" "sugred Sonnets," which were then circulating in manuscript (they were first collected in 1609). Meres describes Shakespeare as "one of the best" English playwrights of both comedy and tragedy. In *Remains . . . Concerning Britain* (1605),

William Camden – a more authoritative source than the imitative Meres – calls Shakespeare one of the "most pregnant witts of these our times" and joins him with such writers as Chapman, Daniel, Jonson, Marston, and Spenser. During the first decades of the seventeenth century, publishers began to attribute numerous play quartos, including some non-Shakespearean ones, to Shakespeare, either by name or initials, and we may assume that they deemed Shakespeare's name and supposed authorship, true or false, commercially attractive.

For the next ten years or so, various records show Shakespeare's dual career as playwright and man of the theater in London, and as an important local figure in Stratford. In 1608-9 his acting company – designated the "King's Men" soon after King James had succeeded Queen Elizabeth in 1603 – rented, refurbished, and opened a small interior playing space, the Blackfriars theater, in London, and Shakespeare was once again listed as a substantial sharer in the group of proprietors of the playhouse. By May 11, 1612, however, he describes himself as a Stratford resident in a London lawsuit – an indication that he had withdrawn from day-to-day professional activity and returned to the town where he had always had his main financial interests. When Shakespeare bought a substantial residential building in London, the Blackfriars Gatehouse, close to the theater of the same name, on March 10, 1613, he is recorded as William Shakespeare "of Stratford upon Avon in the county of Warwick, gentleman," and he named several London residents as the building's trustees. Still, he continued to participate in theatrical activity: when the new Earl of Rutland needed an allegorical design to bear as a shield, or *impresa,* at the celebration of King James's Accession Day, March 24, 1613, the earl's accountant recorded a payment of 44 shillings to Shakespeare for the device with its motto.

For the last few years of his life, Shakespeare evidently

concentrated his activities in the town of his birth. Most of the final records concern business transactions in Stratford, ending with the notation of his death on April 23, 1616, and burial in Holy Trinity Church, Stratford-upon-Avon.

THE QUESTION OF AUTHORSHIP

The history of ascribing Shakespeare's plays (the poems do not come up so often) to someone else began, as it continues, peculiarly. The earliest published claim that someone else wrote Shakespeare's plays appeared in an 1856 article by Delia Bacon in the American journal *Putnam's Monthly* – although an Englishman, Thomas Wilmot, had shared his doubts in private (even secretive) conversations with friends near the end of the eighteenth century. Bacon's was a sad personal history that ended in madness and poverty, but the year after her article, she published, with great difficulty and the bemused assistance of Nathaniel Hawthorne (then United States Consul in Liverpool, England), her *Philosophy of the Plays of Shakspere Unfolded*. This huge, ornately written, confusing farrago is almost unreadable; sometimes its intents, to say nothing of its arguments, disappear entirely beneath near-raving, ecstatic writing. Tumbled in with much supposed "philosophy" appear the claims that Francis Bacon (from whom Delia Bacon eventually claimed descent), Walter Ralegh, and several other contemporaries of Shakespeare's had written the plays. The book had little impact except as a ridiculed curiosity.

Once proposed, however, the issue gained momentum among people whose conviction was the greater in proportion to their ignorance of sixteenth- and seventeenth-century English literature, history, and society. Another American amateur, Catherine P. Ashmead Windle, made the next influential contribution to the cause when she

XX ❧ THE THEATRICAL WORLD

published *Report to the British Museum* (1882), wherein she promised to open "the Cipher of Francis Bacon," though what she mostly offers, in the words of S. Schoenbaum, is "demented allegorizing." An entire new cottage industry grew from Windle's suggestion that the texts contain hidden, cryptographically discoverable ciphers – "clues" – to their authorship; and today there are not only books devoted to the putative ciphers, but also pamphlets, journals, and newsletters.

Although Baconians have led the pack of those seeking a substitute Shakespeare, in *"Shakespeare" Identified* (1920), J. Thomas Looney became the first published "Oxfordian" when he proposed Edward de Vere, seventeenth earl of Oxford, as the secret author of Shakespeare's plays. Also for Oxford and his "authorship" there are today dedicated societies, articles, journals, and books. Less popular candidates – Queen Elizabeth and Christopher Marlowe among them – have had adherents, but the movement seems to have divided into two main contending factions, Baconian and Oxfordian. (For further details on all the candidates for "Shakespeare," see S. Schoenbaum, *Shakespeare's Lives,* 2nd ed., 1991.)

The Baconians, the Oxfordians, and supporters of other candidates have one trait in common – they are snobs. Every pro-Bacon or pro-Oxford tract sooner or later claims that the historical William Shakespeare of Stratford-upon-Avon could not have written the plays because he could not have had the training, the university education, the experience, and indeed the imagination or background their author supposedly possessed. Only a learned genius like Bacon or an aristocrat like Oxford could have written such fine plays. (As it happens, lucky male children of the middle class had access to better education than most aristocrats in Elizabethan England – and Oxford was not particularly well educated.) Shakespeare received in the Stratford grammar school a formal education that would daunt many college graduates today; and popular rival playwrights such as the very learned Ben Jonson and George Chapman, both of whom also lacked university training, achieved great artistic success, without being taken as Bacon or Oxford.

Besides snobbery, one other quality characterizes the authorship controversy: lack of evidence. A great deal of testimony from Shakespeare's time shows that Shakespeare wrote Shakespeare's plays and that his contemporaries recognized them as distinctive and distinctly superior. (Some of that contemporary evidence is collected in E. K. Chambers, *William Shakespeare: A Study of Facts and Problems,* 2 vols., 1930.) Since that testimony comes from Shakespeare's enemies and theatrical competitors as well as from his co-workers and from the Elizabethan equivalent of literary journalists, it seems unlikely that, if any one of these sources had known he was a fraud, they would have failed to record that fact.

Books About Shakespeare's Theater

Useful scholarly studies of theatrical life in Shakespeare's day include: G. E. Bentley, *The Jacobean and Caroline Stage,* 7 vols. (1941-68), and the same author's *The Professions of Dramatist and Player in Shakespeare's Time, 1590-1642* (1986); E. K. Chambers, *The Elizabethan Stage,* 4 vols. (1923); R. A. Foakes, *Illustrations of the English Stage, 1580-1642* (1985); Andrew Gurr, *The Shakespearean Stage,* 3rd ed. (1992), and the same author's *Play-going in Shakespeare's London,* 2nd ed. (1996); Edwin Nungezer, *A Dictionary of Actors* (1929); Carol Chillington Rutter, ed., *Documents of the Rose Playhouse* (1984).

Books About Shakespeare's Life

The following books provide scholarly, documented accounts of Shakespeare's life: G. E. Bentley, *Shakespeare: A Biographical Handbook* (1961); E. K. Chambers, *William Shakespeare: A Study of Facts and Problems,* 2 vols. (1930); S. Schoenbaum, *William Shakespeare: A Compact*

Documentary Life (1977); and *Shakespeare's Lives*, 2nd ed. (1991), by the same author. Many scholarly editions of Shakespeare's complete works print brief compilations of essential dates and events. References to Shakespeare's works up to 1700 are collected in C. M. Ingleby et al., *The Shakespeare Allusion-Book*, rev. ed., 2 vols. (1932).

The Texts of Shakespeare

As FAR AS WE KNOW, only one manuscript conceivably in Shakespeare's own hand may (and even this is much disputed) exist: a few pages of a play called *Sir Thomas More,* which apparently was never performed. What we do have, as later readers, performers, scholars, students, are printed texts. The earliest of these survive in two forms: quartos and folios. Quartos (from the Latin for "four") are small books, printed on sheets of paper that were then folded in fours, to make eight double-sided pages. When these were bound together, the result was a squarish, eminently portable volume that sold for the relatively small sum of sixpence (translating in modern terms to about $5.00). In folios, on the other hand, the sheets are folded only once, in half, producing large, impressive volumes taller than they are wide. This was the format for important works of philosophy, science, theology, and literature (the major precedent for a folio Shakespeare was Ben Jonson's *Works,* 1616). The decision to print the works of a popular playwright in folio is an indication of how far up on the social scale the theatrical profession had come during Shakespeare's lifetime. The Shakespeare folio was an expensive book, selling for between fifteen and eighteen shillings, depending on the binding (in modern terms, from about $150 to $180). Twenty Shakespeare plays of the thirty-seven that survive first appeared in quarto, seventeen of which appeared during Shakespeare's lifetime; the rest of the plays are found only in folio.

The First Folio was published in 1623, seven years after Shakespeare's death, and was authorized by his fellow actors, the co-owners of the King's Men. This publication was certainly a mark of the company's enormous respect for Shakespeare; but it was also a way of turning the old plays, most of which were no longer current in the playhouse, into ready money (the folio includes only Shakespeare's plays, not his sonnets or other nondramatic verse). Whatever the motives behind the publication of the folio, the texts it preserves constitute the basis for almost all later editions of the playwright's works. The texts, however, differ from those of the earlier quartos, sometimes in minor respects but often significantly – most strikingly in the two texts of *King Lear,* but also in important ways in *Hamlet, Othello,* and *Troilus and Cressida.* (The variants are recorded in the textual notes to each play in the new Pelican series.) The differences in these texts represent, in a sense, the essence of theater: the texts of plays were initially not intended for publication. They were scripts, designed for the actors to perform – the principal life of the play at this period was in performance. And it follows that in Shakespeare's theater the playwright typically had no say either in how his play was performed or in the disposition of his text – he was an employee of the company. The authoritative figures in the theatrical enterprise were the shareholders in the company, who were for the most part the major actors. They decided what plays were to be done; they hired the playwright and often gave him an outline of the play they wanted him to write. Often, too, the play was a collaboration: the company would retain a group of writers, and parcel out the scenes among them. The resulting script was then the property of the company, and the actors would revise it as they saw fit during the course of putting it on stage. The resulting text belonged to the company. The playwright had no rights in it once he had been paid. (This system survives largely intact in the movie industry, and most of the playwrights of Shakespeare's time were as anonymous as most screenwriters are today.) The script could also, of course, continue to change as the tastes of audiences and the requirements of the actors changed. Many – perhaps most – plays were re-vised when they were reintroduced after any substantial absence from the repertory, or when they were performed by a company different from the one that originally com-missioned the play.

Shakespeare was an exceptional figure in this world because he was not only a shareholder and actor in his company, but also its leading playwright – he was literally his own boss. He had, moreover, little interest in the publication of his plays, and even those that appeared during his lifetime with the authorization of the company show no signs of any editorial concern on the part of the author. Theater was, for Shakespeare, a fluid and supremely responsive medium – the very opposite of the great classic canonical text that has embodied his works since 1623.

The very fluidity of the original texts, however, has meant that Shakespeare has always had to be edited. Here is an example of how problematic the editorial pro-ject inevitably is, a passage from the most famous speech in *Romeo and Juliet,* Juliet's balcony soliloquy beginning "O Romeo, Romeo, wherefore art thou Romeo?" Since the eighteenth century, the standard modern text has read,

> What's Montague? It is nor hand, nor foot,
> Nor arm, nor face, nor any other part
> Belonging to a man. O be some other name!
> What's in a name? That which we call a rose
> By any other name would smell as sweet.
> (II.2.40-44)

Editors have three early texts of this play to work from, two quarto texts and the folio. Here is how the First Quarto (1597) reads:

> Whats *Mountague?* It is nor band nor foote,
> Nor arme, nor face, nor any other part.
> Whats in a name? That which we call a Rofe,
> By any other name would fmell as fweet:

Here is the Second Quarto (1599):

> Whats *Mountague?* it is nor hand nor foote,
> Nor arme nor face, ô be fome other name
> Belonging to a man.
> Whats in a name that which we call a rofe,
> By any other word would fmell as fweete,

And here is the First Folio (1623):

> What's *Mountague?* it is nor hand nor foote,
> Nor arme, nor face, O be fome other name
> Belonging to a man.
> What? in a names that which we call a Rofe,
> By any other word would fmell as fweete,

There is in fact no early text that reads as our modern text does – and this is the most famous speech in the play. Instead, we have three quite different texts, all of which are clearly some version of the same speech, but none of which seems to us a final or satisfactory version. The transcendently beautiful passage in modern editions is an editorial invention: editors have succeeded in conflating and revising the three versions into something we recognize as great poetry. Is this what Shakespeare "really" wrote? Who can say? What we can say is that Shakespeare always had performance, not a book, in mind.

Books About the Shakespeare Texts

The standard study of the printing history of the First Folio is W. W. Greg, *The Shakespeare First Folio* (1955). J. K. Walton, *The Quarto Copy for the First Folio of Shakespeare* (1971), is a useful survey of the relation of the quartos to the folio. The second edition of Charlton Hinman's *Norton Facsimile* of the First Folio (1996), with a new introduction by Peter Blayney, is indispensable. Stanley Wells and Gary Taylor, *William Shakespeare: A Textual Companion,* keyed to the Oxford text, gives a comprehensive survey of the editorial situation for all the plays and poems.

THE GENERAL EDITORS

Introduction

SHAKESPEARE'S SCOTTISH TRAGEDY was written early in the reign of James I, the Scottish king who succeeded Queen Elizabeth on the English throne in 1603. It is impossible to date the play precisely, but certain allusions – especially to the Gunpowder Plot, the Jesuit attempt to blow up Parliament in 1605, and the subsequent trial of the conspirators – suggest a date in 1606. The impulse to write a Scottish play must have been in the broadest sense political: the king who had, as one of his first official acts, taken Shakespeare's company under his patronage, so that the Lord Chamberlain's Men became the King's Men, traced his ancestry back to Banquo. But there is little about the play to suggest that Shakespeare's purpose was to celebrate his patron's lineage, just as there is nothing straightforward about the history Shakespeare chose to dramatize.

The play, moreover, comes to us not as it would have appeared from Shakespeare's pen in 1606, but in a version that is demonstrably a revision; and the reviser was certainly not Shakespeare. It includes songs for the witches that are given in the text only with their opening words ("Come away, come away, etc."; "Black spirits, etc."). These are songs from Thomas Middleton's play *The Witch,* written between 1610 and 1615, where they constitute little divertissements, sung dialogues with dances. The manuscript of Sir William Davenant's version of *Macbeth,* prepared around 1664, includes the whole text of the witches' songs from Middleton, and since *The Witch* remained unpublished until 1778, Davenant would have taken his text not from Middleton, but directly from the King's Men's performing text of *Macbeth,* to which Davenant had acquired the rights. This, then, is the earliest version of the play to which we have access, the play as the King's Men were performing it shortly after Shakespeare's death – for whatever reason, they chose not to return to Shakespeare's original text when they published the 1623 First Folio. The present edition includes the whole of the two witch scenes – what is implied in the folio's "etc."

The play as it stands in the folio is anomalous in a number of other respects as well. Textually it is very unusual: by far the shortest of the tragedies (half the length of *Hamlet,* a third shorter than the average), shorter, too, than all the comedies except *The Comedy of Errors.* It looks, moreover, as if the version we have has not only been augmented with witches' business, but also cut and rearranged, producing some real muddles in the narrative: for example, the scene between Lennox and the Lord, III.6, reporting action that has not happened yet, or the notorious syntactic puzzles of the account of the battle in the opening scenes, or the confusion of the final battle, in which Macbeth is slain onstage, and twenty lines later Macduff reenters with his head. Revision and cutting were, of course, standard and necessary procedures in a theater where the normal playing time was two hours; but if theatrical cuts are to explain the peculiarities of this text, why was it cut so peculiarly, not to say ineptly? Arguments that make the muddles not the result of cutting but an experiment in surreal and expressionistic dramaturgy only produce more questions, rendering the play a total anomaly, both in Shakespeare's work and in the drama of the period.

The elaboration of the witches' roles could have taken place anywhere up to about fifteen years after the play was first performed, but the presence of the Middleton songs suggests that Shakespeare was no longer around to do the revising, which presumes a date after 1614. Why, only a decade after the play was written, would augmenting the witches' roles have seemed a good idea? To begin with, by 1610 or so witchcraft, magic, and the diabolical were good theater business. Ben Jonson's *Masque of Queens,* performed at court in 1609, opens on a witches' coven with infernal music and dance, and inaugurated a decade of sorcery plays and masques, of which the most famous are *The Tempest, The Alchemist,* and the revived and rewritten *Doctor Faustus.*

The ubiquitousness of theatrical magic is perhaps sufficient reason for the elaboration of the witches in *Macbeth,* but it does not seem to account for everything. When Macbeth, after the murder of Banquo, goes to consult the witches, and they show him a terrifying vision of Banquo's heirs, the chief witch Hecate proposes a little entertainment to cheer him up:

> I'll charm the air to give a sound
> While you perform your antic round,
> That this great king may kindly say
> Our duties did his welcome pay
> (IV.1.151-54)

The tone of the scene here changes significantly: the witches are not professional and peremptory anymore; they are lighthearted, gracious, and deferential. We may choose to treat this as a moment of heavy irony, though Macbeth does not seem to respond to it as such; but if it is not ironic, the change of tone suggests that the "great king" addressed in this passage is not the king onstage, but instead a real king in the audience, Banquo's descendant and the king of both Scotland and England. If this is correct, then the version of the play preserved in the folio is one prepared for a performance at court.

Though there is no record of a court performance, King James surely must have wanted to see a play that included both witches and his ancestors. Indeed, whether or not King James was in the audience, the fact that it is the witches who provide the royal entertainment can hardly be accidental. The king was intensely interested in witchcraft. He attended witch trials whenever he could, and considered himself an expert on the theory and practice of sorcery. His dialogue on the subject, *Dæmonology,* first published in Edinburgh in 1597, was reissued (three times) upon his accession to the English throne in 1603. This and the *Basilicon Doron,* his philosophy of kingship, were the two works through which he chose to introduce himself to his English subjects: witchcraft and kingship have an intimate relationship in the Jacobean royal ideology.

The presence of the witches is another unusual, if not quite anomalous, feature of the play. Shakespeare makes use of the supernatural from time to time – ghosts in *Richard III,* in *Julius Caesar,* and most notably in *Hamlet;* fairies and their magic in *A Midsummer Night's Dream;* Prospero's sorcery in *The Tempest;* Joan of Arc's and Marjory Jourdain's in the *Henry VI* plays; and Rosalind's claim to be a magician at the end of *As You Like It* – but there is no other play in which witches and witchcraft are such an integral element of the plot. This is a culture in which the supernatural and witchcraft, even for skeptics, are as much a part of reality as religious truth is. Like the ghost in *Hamlet,* the reality of the witches in Macbeth is not in question; the question, as in *Hamlet,* is why they are present and how far to believe them.

Like the ghost, too, the witches are quintessential theatrical devices: they dance and sing, perform wonders, appear and disappear, fly, produce visions – do, in short, all the things that, historically, we have gone to the theater to see. They open the play and set the tone for it. On Shakespeare's stage they would simply have materialized through a trapdoor, but Shakespeare's audience believed in magic already. Our rationalistic theater requires something more theatrically elaborate – not necessarily machinery, but some serious mystification. For Shakespeare's audience, the mystification is built into their physical appearance, which defies the categories: they look like men and are women. The indeterminacy of their gender is the first thing Banquo calls attention to. This is a defining element of their nature, a paradox that identifies them as witches: a specifically female propensity to evil – being a witch – is defined by its apparent masculinity. This also is, of course, one of the central charges leveled at Shakespeare's theater itself, the ambiguity of its gender roles, the fact that on Shakespeare's stage the women are really male. But the gender ambiguity relates as well to roles within the play: Lady Macbeth unsexes herself, and accuses her husband of being afraid to act like a man. What constitutes acting like a man in this play? The answer would seem to be, only killing. Lady Macbeth unsexing herself, after all, renders herself, unexpectedly, not a man but a child, and thus incapable of murder: "Had he not resembled / My father as he slept, I had done't" (II.2.12-13). Indeed, the definitive relation between murder and manhood applies to heroes as well as villains. When Macduff is told of the murder of his wife and children and is urged to "Dispute it like a man," he replies that he must first "feel it as a man" (IV.3.221-23). Whatever this says about his sensitivity and family feeling, it also says that murder is what makes you feel like a man.

The unsettling quality of the witches goes beyond gender. Their language is paradoxical – fair is foul and foul is fair; when the battle's lost and won. One way of looking at this is to say that it constitutes no paradox at all: any battle that is lost has also been won, but by somebody else. The person who describes a battle as lost and won is either on both sides or on neither; what is fair for one side is bound to be foul for the other. The witches' riddles and prophecies mislead Macbeth, but in an important sense, these double-talking creatures are also telling the truth about the world of the play – that there really are no ethical standards in it, no right and wrong sides. Duncan certainly starts out sounding like a good king: the rhetoric of his monarchy is full of claims about its sacredness, the deference that is due to it, how it is part of a natural hierarchy descending from God, how the king is divinely anointed, and so forth. But in fact none of this is borne out by the play. Duncan's rule is utterly chaotic, and maintaining it depends on constant warfare – the battle that opens the play, after all, is not an invasion, but a rebellion. Duncan's rule has never commanded the deference it claims for itself – deference is not natural to it. In upsetting that sense of the deference Macbeth feels he owes to Duncan, perhaps the witches are releasing into the play something the play both overtly denies and implicitly articulates: that there is no basis whatever for the values asserted on Duncan's behalf; that the primary characteristic of his rule, perhaps of any rule in the world of the play, is not order but rebellion.

Whether or not this is correct, it must be to the point that women are the ones who prompt this dangerous realization in Macbeth. The witches live outside the social order, but they embody its contradictions: beneath the woman's exterior is also a man, just as beneath the man's exterior is also a woman; nature is anarchic, full of competing claims, not ordered and hierarchical. To acknowledge our divided selves and the anarchy of nature is also to acknowledge the reality and force and validity of the individual will – to acknowledge that all of us have claims that conflict with the claims about natural order, deference, and hierarchy. This is the same recognition that Edmund brings into *King Lear* when he invokes Nature as his goddess. It is a Nature that is not the image of divine order, but one in which the strongest and craftiest survive – and when they survive, they then go on to devise claims about Nature that justify their success, claims about hierarchies, natural law and order, the divine right of kings. Edmund is a villain, but if he were ultimately successful, he would be indistinguishable from the Duncans and Malcolms (and James I's) of Shakespeare's world.

The complexities and ambiguities of Shakespeare's story are firmly based on history. The real Macbeth was, like Richard III, the victim of a gigantic and very effective publicity campaign. Historically, Duncan was the usurper – that is what the rebellion at the beginning of the play is about, though there is no way of knowing it from Shakespeare. Macbeth had a claim to the throne (Duncan at one point in the play refers to him as "cousin" [I.4.14] – they were first cousins, both grandsons of King Malcolm II). Macbeth's murder of Duncan was a political assassination, and Macbeth was a popular hero because of it. The legitimate heir to the throne, whose rights have been displaced by the usurping Duncan, was Lady Macbeth. When Macbeth ascended the throne, he was ruling as Protector or Regent until Lady Macbeth's son came of age (she did have children – it is Shakespeare who deprives her and Macbeth of those heirs). Macbeth's defeat at the end of the play, by Malcolm, Macduff, and Siward, the Earl of Northumberland, constituted essentially an English invasion – the long-term fight was between native Scottish Celts and Anglo-Norman invaders, with continental allies (such as the Norwegian king) on both sides. One way of looking at the action is to say that it is about the enforced anglicization of Scotland, which Macbeth is resisting.

Shakespeare knows some of this. In Holinshed's *Chronicles,* from which Shakespeare took his history, Macbeth not only has a claim to the throne, he also has a legitimate grievance against Duncan. Moreover, in Holinshed, Banquo is fully Macbeth's accomplice, and the murder of Duncan has a good deal of political justification. All this would be very touchy for Shakespeare precisely because Banquo is King James's ancestor, and if Duncan is a saint, then Banquo is a real problem, the ancestor one wants to forget. In fact, Banquo's connection with the Scottish royal line materializes only two centuries after the events of the play, when one of his descendants, a steward in the royal household, married into the royal family – hence King James's family name, Stewart or Stuart. Shakespeare's way of handling Banquo fudges a lot of issues. Should he not, as a loyal thane, be pressing the claim of Malcolm, the designated heir, after the murder? Should he remain loyal to Macbeth as long as he does?

This is precisely the sort of question that shows how close the play is to *Hamlet:* in both plays, the issue of legitimacy remains crucially ambiguous. Nobody in *Macbeth* presses the claim of Malcolm until Malcolm reappears with an army to support him, any more than anyone in *Hamlet* presses the claim of Hamlet. In both plays, there is deep uncertainty about the relation between power and legitimacy – about whether legitimacy constitutes anything more than the rhetoric of power backed by the size of its army. Duncan tries to legitimize his son's succession by creating Malcolm Prince of Cumberland on the analogy of the Prince of Wales, thus declaring him heir to the throne. But this is not the way the succession works in Scotland: Cumberland is an *English* county, which was briefly ceded to the Scottish crown, and Malcolm's new title is the thin edge of the English invasion. Analogously, Malcolm confirms his victory at the end of the play by transforming his Scottish thanes into English earls, "the first that ever Scotland / In such an honor named" (V.8.63-64) – heredity requires a great deal of ceremonial apparatus to make it appear a natural mode of succession. James I himself became king of England not because he was the legitimate heir (he was one of a number of people with a distant claim to the throne), but because he was *designated* the successor by Queen Elizabeth; or at least several attendants at her death claimed that he was, and the people in control supported him. This is much closer to the situation in *Hamlet* and *Macbeth* than it is to any system of hereditary succession. And Macbeth is, even in the play, a fully legitimate king, as legitimate as Duncan: like Hamlet's Denmark, this is not a hereditary monarchy. Macbeth is *elected* king by the thanes, and duly anointed. The fact that he turns out to be a bad king does not make him any less the king, any more than the rebellion that opens the play casts doubt on Duncan's right to the throne.

The play is less about legitimacy and usurpation than about the divided self, and like *Hamlet,* it focuses to an unprecedented extent on the mind of the hero. Suppose we try to imagine a *Hamlet* written from Claudius's point of view, in the way that *Macbeth* is written from Macbeth's. The murder Claudius commits is the perfect crime; but the hero-villain quickly finds that his actions have unimagined implications, and that the political world is not all he has to contend with. As it stands, *Hamlet* is a very political play, and does not really need the ghost at all. Hamlet has his suspicions already; Claudius tries to buy him off by promising him the succession, but this is not good enough. It turns out that the problem is not really conscience or revenge, it is Hamlet's own ambitions. He wanted to succeed his father on the throne; Claudius, Hamlet says, "lept in between the election and my hopes." The ghost is merely a deus ex machina. But in a *Hamlet* that did not center on Hamlet, Claudius's guilty conscience, which is not much in evidence in the play, would have a great deal more work to do. So would the ghost – who should, after all, logically be haunting Claudius, not Hamlet. This play would be not about politics but about how the dead do not disappear; they return to embody our crimes, so that we have to keep repeating them – just as in *Macbeth*. In this version of *Hamlet,* Hamlet is hardly necessary, any more than in *Macbeth,* Malcolm and Macduff are necessary. The drama of Macbeth is really a matter between Macbeth and his ambition, Macbeth and the witches and his wife and his hallucinations and his own tortured soul, the drama of prophecies and riddles, and how he understands them, and what he decides to do about them, and how they, in themselves, constitute retribution.

What, then, about the riddles, those verbal incarnations of the imperfect speakers the witches? Macbeth is told that he will never be conquered till Birnam Wood comes to Dunsinane; and that no man of woman born will harm him. Are these paradoxical impossibilities realized? Not at all, really: the Birnam Wood prophecy does not come true, it just appears to Macbeth that it does – the wood is not moving, it merely looks as if it is. Or alternatively, we could say that "Birnam Wood" is a quibble: Macbeth assumes it means the forest, but it could mean merely wood from the forest, the branches the soldiers are using for camouflage – the prophecy comes true merely as a stage device. As for "no man of woman born," maybe the problem is that Macbeth is not a close enough reader: he takes the operative word to be "woman" – "No man of *woman* born shall harm Macbeth" – but the key word turns out to be "born" – "No man of woman *born* shall harm Macbeth." If this is right, we must go on to consider the implications of the assumption that a cesarean section does not constitute birth. This is really, historically, quite significant: a vaginal birth would have been handled by women – the midwife, maids, attendants – with no men present. But surgery was a male prerogative – the surgeon was always a man; midwives were not allowed to use surgical instruments – and the surgical birth thus means, in Renaissance terms, that Macduff was brought to life by men, not women: carried by a woman, but made viable only through masculine intervention. Such a birth, all but invariably, involved the mother's death.

Macbeth himself sees it this way, when he defies Macduff and says,

> Though Birnam Wood be come to Dunsinane,
> And thou opposed, being of no woman born
>
> (V.8.30–31)

where logically it should be "being not of woman born": the key concept is not "no woman," but "not born." But Shakespeare seems to be conceiving of a masculine equivalent to the immaculate conception, a birth uncontaminated by women, as the Virgin's was uncontaminated by man.

So this riddle bears on the whole issue of the place of women in the play's world, and especially on how very disruptive they seem to be, even when, like Lady Macduff, they are loving and nurturing. Why is it so important, for example, at the end of the play, that Malcolm is a virgin? Malcolm insists to Macduff that he is utterly pure, "yet / Unknown to woman" (IV.3.125-26), uncontaminated by heterosexuality – this is offered as the first of his qualifications for displacing and succeeding Macbeth. Perhaps this bears too on the really big unanswered question about Macduff: why he left his family unprotected when he went to seek Malcolm in England – this is what makes Malcolm mistrust him so deeply. Why would you leave your wife and children unprotected, to face the tyrant's rage, unless you knew they were really in no danger?

But somehow the question goes unanswered, does not need to be answered, perhaps because Lady Macduff in some way is the problem, just as, more obviously, Lady Macbeth and the witches are. Those claims on Macduff that tie him to his wife and children, that would keep him at home, that purport to be higher than the claims of masculine solidarity, are in fact rejected quite decisively by the play. In Holinshed, Macduff flees only *after* his wife and children have been murdered, and therefore for the best of reasons. Macduff's desertion of his family is Shakespeare's addition to the story. Maybe, the play keeps saying, if it weren't for all those women? The play is very much a masculinist, even misogynistic, fantasy, especially at the end, when there are simply no women left, not even the witches, and the restored commonwealth is a world of heroic soldiers.

So, to return to the increasingly elaborate witches'
scenes, the first thing they do for this claustrophobic play
is to open up a space for women; and it is a subversive and
paradoxical space. This is a play in which paradoxes
abound, and for Shakespeare's audience, Lady Macbeth
would have embodied those paradoxes as powerfully as
the witches do: in her proclaimed ability to "unsex" herself, in her willingness to dash her own infant's brains out,
but most of all, in the kind of control she exercises over
her husband. The marriage at the center of the play is one
of the most frightening things about it, but it is worth ob-
serving that, as Shakespearean marriages go, this is a good
one: intense, intimate, loving. The notion that your wife
is your friend and your comfort is not a Shakespearean one. The relaxed, easygoing, happy times men and
women have together in Shakespeare all take place before
marriage, as part of the wooing process – this is the subject of comedy. What happens after marriage is the subject of tragedy – King Lear's wicked daughters Goneril
and Regan are only extreme versions of perfectly norma-
tive Shakespearean wives. The only Shakespearean marriage of any duration that is represented as specifically
sexually happy is the marriage of Claudius and Gertrude,
a murderer and an adulteress; and it is probably to the
point that even they stop sleeping together after only four
months – not, to be sure, by choice.

In this context, Macbeth and Lady Macbeth are really
quite well matched. They care for each other and understand each other deeply, exhibiting a genuine intimacy
and trust of a sort one does not find, for example, in the
marriage of the Capulets, or in Iago and Emilia (to say
nothing of Othello and Desdemona), or in Coriolanus
and Virgilia, or in Cymbeline and his villainous queen
(who is not even provided with a name), or in Leontes
and Hermione. The prospects for life after marriage in
Shakespeare are pretty grim. And in this respect, probably

the most frightening thing in the play is the genuine power of Lady Macbeth's mind, her powers of both analysis and persuasion, and even more her intimate apprehension of her husband's deepest desires, her perfect understanding of what combination of arguments will prove irresistible to the masculine ego: "Be a man," and "If you really loved me you'd do it."

But can the play's action really be accounted for simply by the addition of yet another witch? Macbeth's marriage is a version of the Adam and Eve story, the woman persuading the man to commit the primal sin against the father. But the case is loaded: surely Lady Macbeth is not the culprit, any more than Eve is – or than the witches are. What she does is give voice to Macbeth's inner life, release in him the same forbidden desire that the witches have called forth. To act on this desire is what it means in the play to be a man. But having evoked her husband's murderous ambition, having dared him to stop being a child, she suddenly finds that when he *is* a man, she is powerless. Her own power was only her power over the child, the child she was willing to destroy to gain the power of a man.

Performers and revisers from the late seventeenth century on have never been happy with the way Lady Macbeth simply fades out, and Macbeth is perfunctorily killed. The play does not even provide its hero with a final speech, let alone a eulogy for Shakespeare's most complex and brilliant studies in villainy. Malcolm dismisses the pair succinctly as "this dead butcher and his fiendlike queen." Sir William Davenant, refurbishing the play for Restoration audiences, added a rather awkward dying line for Macbeth ("Farewell vain world, and what's most vain in it, ambition"), and tastefully resolved the problem of Macbeth's double death by leaving the body onstage and having Macduff reenter with Macbeth's sword, instead of his head. By the mid-eighteenth century, David Garrick –

who was claiming to be performing the play "as written by Shakespeare" – had inserted an extended death speech for the hero:

> 'Tis done! The scene of life will quickly close.
> Ambition's vain, delusive dreams are fled,
> And now I wake to darkness, guilt and horror;
> I cannot bear it! Let me shake it off –
> 'Twill not be; my soul is clogged with blood –
> I cannot rise! I dare not ask for mercy –
> It is too late, hell drags me down; I sink,
> I sink – Oh! – my soul is lost forever!
> Oh!

This Faustian peroration went on being used until well into the nineteenth century.

The one element that has always proved satisfying in Shakespeare's ending is the clear and unambiguous triumph of good over evil. But there is a puzzling aspect to the conclusion, which is less symmetrical and more open-ended than this suggests. Why, in a play so clearly organized around ideas of good and evil, is it not Malcolm who defeats Macbeth – the incarnation of virtue, the man who has never told a lie or slept with a woman, overcoming the monster of vice? In fact, historically, this is what happened: Macbeth was killed in battle by Malcolm, not Macduff. Shakespeare is following Holinshed here, but why, especially in a play that revises so much else in its source material? Davenant recognizes this as a problem, and, followed by Garrick, gives Macduff a few lines of justification as he kills Macbeth:

> This for thy Royal master Duncan
> This for my dearest friend my wife,
> This for those pledges of our loves my children . . .
> I'll as a trophy bear away his sword
> To witness my revenge.

The addition is significant, and revealing: in Shakespeare, Macduff, fulfilling the prophecy, is simply acting as Malcolm's agent, the man not born of woman acting for the king uncontaminated by women. But why does virtue need an agent, while vice can act for itself? And what about the agent: does the unanswered question about Macduff abandoning his family not linger in the back of our minds? Does his willingness to condone the vices Malcolm invents for himself not say something disturbing about the quality of Macduff as a hero? Is he not, in fact, the pragmatic soldier who does what needs to be done so that the saintly king can stay clear of the complexities and paradoxes of politics and war? And what happens next, with a saintly king of Scotland, and an ambitious soldier as his right-hand man, and those threatening offspring, the heirs of Banquo, still waiting in the wings?

STEPHEN ORGEL
Stanford University

Note on the Text

THIS EDITION IS, with the two exceptions indicated below, based on the only substantive text, the folio of 1623. This apparently derived from a transcript of the promptbook, which preserved a revised version of the play, including some non-Shakespearean elements (see the Introduction). The act and scene division here supplied coincides with that of the folio text except that V.7 of the latter is here subdivided into scenes 7 and 8. (Another possible point of subdivision comes at V.8.35, and is marked by some editors as scene 9.) The following list of emendations records the only substantive departures from the folio text; however, the lineation in the folio is unusually erratic, and relineation has not been recorded. The readings in this edition are in italics, the folio readings in roman.

I.1 **10–13** SECOND WITCH . . . *air* (in F these lines form a single speech attributed to "All")

I.2 **13** *galloglasses* Gallowgrosses **14** *quarrel* Quarry (a variant spelling of "quarrel")

I.3 **32** *weïrd* weyward (so throughout) **39** *Forres* Soris (The town is named Forres. The error is Holinshed's, like the S/F error in Macbeth's father's name at line 71.) **71** *Finel* Sinel (his name was Finel or Finley; another S/F error from Holinshed) **98** *Came* Can **109** *borrowed* borrowèd

I.4 **1** *Are* Or

I.5 **46** *it* hit (a variant spelling)

I.6 **4** *martlet* Barlet **5** *loved* lovèd **9** *most* must **27** *count* compt (a variant spelling)

I.7 **6** *shoal* Schoole (a variant spelling) **47** *do* no

II.1 **56** *side* sides (Pope's emendation "strides" has been almost universally adopted, but it is bibliographically unsound – a compositor would not have misread "strides" as "sides" – and both neatens and contradicts the sense: a "stealthy pace" does not "stride." "Sides" is undeniably puzzling, but so is much else in the play. As it stands, it can mean "loins," or, as a verb, "sides with." If the word is to be emended, a more plausible reading would be "side," arrogance – the OED records the noun only in modern examples, but adjectival usages date from the early sixteenth century, and Shakespeare often uses adjectives as substantives. There is a possible parallel in *Coriolanus* I.1.193: Martius claims the plebeians "presume to know / What's done i'th Capitoll: Who's like to rise, / Who thriues, & who declines: Side factions, & give out / Coniecturall Marriages. . . ." "Side" is always taken as a verb here – they will favor certain factions – but syntactically the adjectival use is more likely: they will pretend to know which factions are arrogant, guilty of their own vice of presumptuousness. "Sides" for "side" is, moreover, a plausible compositor's error: the tail of a final e in secretary hand is easily misread as a final s.)   **57** *sure* sowre   **58** *way they* they may

II.2 13 s.d. *Enter Macbeth* (after line 8 in F)

II.3 79 *horror* (F adds "Ring the bell," but the bell has already been called for at line 73, and is rung, logically, as soon as the speech is finished. As Theobald observed, this looks like the prompter's marginal instruction to himself, and Lady Macbeth's line metrically completes the verse.)

III.1 62 *grip* gripe (a variant spelling)

III.4 41 s.d. F has the ghost enter at line 37; but he logically enters when he is summoned (as at line 92 also)   **79** *time* times   **92 s.d.** After line 89 in F   **136** *worst. For* worst, for   **145** *in deed* indeed

III.5 35ff. F reads,

> Hearke, I am call'd: my little Spirit see
> Sits in a Foggy cloud, and stayes for me
>   *Sing within. Come away, come away, &c.*
> I. Come, Let's make hast, shee'l soone be
> Backe againe.   *Exeunt.*

My text is edited from the ms of Davenant's *Macbeth,* which apparently derives from the King's Men's prompt copy. See the Introduction.

III.6 24 *son* Sonnes   **38** *the* their

IV.1 43 s.d. F reads, *Musicke and a Song. Blacke Spirits, &c.* See the Introduction.   **81** *all together* altogether   **115** *Dunsinane* Dunsmane   **120** *Birnam* Byrnan   **133 s.d.** *Kings and Banquo, last* Kings, and Banquo last   **141** *eighth* eight

IV.2 22 *none* move   **30 s.d.** *Exit* Exit Rosse   **73 s.d.** *Exit* Exit Messenger   **83** *shag-haired* shagge-ear'd

IV.3 15 *deserve* discerne   **107** *accursed* accust   **133** *thy here-approach* they here approach   **235** *tune* time

V.1 1 *two* too

V.2 5, 31 *Birnam* Byrnan

V.3 2, 62 *Birnam* Byrnan   **41** *Cure her* cure   **57** *senna* Cyme

V.4 3 *Birnam* Byrnan

V.5 34, 44 *Birnam* Byrnan   **39** *shalt* shall

V.7 19 *unbattered* unbatterèd

V.8 30 *Birnam* Byrnan

Macbeth

[NAMES OF THE ACTORS

DUNCAN, *King of Scotland*
MALCOLM $\Big\}$ *his sons*
DONALBAIN
MACBETH
BANQUO
MACDUFF
LENNOX
ROSS $\Big\}$ *Scottish thanes*
MENTEITH
ANGUS
CAITHNESS
FLEANCE, *son to Banquo*
SIWARD, *Earl of Northumberland*
YOUNG SIWARD, *his son*
SEYTON, *an officer attending on Macbeth*
BOY, *son to Macduff*
A CAPTAIN
AN ENGLISH DOCTOR
A SCOTTISH DOCTOR
A PORTER
AN OLD MAN
THREE MURDERERS
LADY MACBETH
LADY MACDUFF
A GENTLEWOMAN, *attending on Lady Macbeth*
THE WEÏRD SISTERS, *witches*
HECATE
APPARITIONS
LORDS, OFFICERS, SOLDIERS, MESSENGERS, ATTENDANTS

SCENE: *Scotland and England*]
*

Macbeth

〜 **I.1** *Thunder and lightning. Enter three Witches.*

FIRST WITCH
  When shall we three meet again?
  In thunder, lightning, or in rain?
SECOND WITCH
  When the hurly-burly's done,   3
  When the battle's lost and won.
THIRD WITCH   That will be ere the set of sun.
FIRST WITCH   Where the place?
SECOND WITCH   Upon the heath.
THIRD WITCH   There to meet with Macbeth.
FIRST WITCH   I come, Graymalkin!   9
SECOND WITCH   Paddock calls.   10
THIRD WITCH   Anon!   11
ALL
  Fair is foul, and foul is fair.
  Hover through the fog and filthy air.   *Exeunt.*
                          *

I.1 An open field **3** *hurly-burly* turmoil **9** *Graymalkin* gray cat, her familiar spirit **10** *Paddock* toad **11** *Anon* at once

∾ **I.2** *Alarum within. Enter King [Duncan], Malcolm,*
     Donalbain, Lennox, with Attendants, meeting a
     bleeding Captain.

KING DUNCAN
     What bloody man is that? He can report,
     As seemeth by his plight, of the revolt
3   The newest state.

MALCOLM   This is the sergeant
     Who like a good and hardy soldier fought
     'Gainst my captivity. Hail, brave friend;
     Say to the king the knowledge of the broil
     As thou didst leave it.

CAPTAIN   Doubtful it stood,
     As two spent swimmers that do cling together
     And choke their art. The merciless Macdonwald –
10   Worthy to be a rebel, for to that
     The multiplying villainies of nature
12   Do swarm upon him – from the Western Isles
13   Of kerns and galloglasses is supplied;
     And Fortune, on his damnèd quarrel smiling,
     Showed like a rebel's whore. But all's too weak:
     For brave Macbeth – well he deserves that name –
     Disdaining Fortune, with his brandished steel,
     Which smoked with bloody execution,
19   Like valor's minion carved out his passage
20   Till he faced the slave;
     Which ne'er shook hands nor bade farewell to him
22   Till he unseamed him from the nave to th' chaps
     And fixed his head upon our battlements.

KING DUNCAN
     O valiant cousin, worthy gentleman!

———

I.2 Duncan's camp **s.d.** *within* offstage   **3** *sergeant* (generic term for a military officer; he ranks as a captain)   **10** *to that* to that end   **12** *Western Isles*
the Hebrides and Ireland   **13** *kerns and galloglasses* Irish mercenary soldiers
19 *minion* darling   **22** *nave* navel; *chaps* jaws

CAPTAIN
  As whence the sun 'gins his reflection
  Shipwracking storms and direful thunders,
  So from that spring whence comfort seemed to come
  Discomfort swells. Mark, King of Scotland, mark.
  No sooner justice had, with valor armed,
  Compelled these skipping kerns to trust their heels   *30*
  But the Norwegian lord, surveying vantage,   *31*
  With furbished arms and new supplies of men,
  Began a fresh assault.
KING DUNCAN   Dismayed not this
  Our captains, Macbeth and Banquo?
CAPTAIN   Yes,
  As sparrows eagles, or the hare the lion.
  If I say sooth, I must report they were
  As cannons overcharged with double cracks,   *37*
  So they doubly redoubled strokes upon the foe.
  Except they meant to bathe in reeking wounds,   *39*
  Or memorize another Golgotha,   *40*
  I cannot tell –
  But I am faint; my gashes cry for help.
KING DUNCAN
  So well thy words become thee as thy wounds,
  They smack of honor both. Go get him surgeons.
                       [Exit Captain, attended.]
      Enter Ross and Angus.
  Who comes here?   *45*
MALCOLM   The worthy Thane of Ross.
LENNOX
  What a haste looks through his eyes! So should he look   *46*
  That seems to speak things strange.   *47*
ROSS   God save the king.

---

31 *surveying vantage* seeing an opportunity   **37** *cracks* explosives   **39** *Except* unless   **40** *memorize another Golgotha* make as memorable as Calvary (where the Crucifixion took place)   **45** *Thane* (a Scottish lord, equivalent to the English earl)   **46** *looks through* appears in   **47** *seems to* is ready to

KING DUNCAN
Whence cam'st thou, worthy thane?
ROSS   From Fife, great king,
Where the Norwegian banners flout the sky
50 And fan our people cold.
51 Norway himself, with terrible numbers,
Assisted by that most disloyal traitor
53 The Thane of Cawdor, began a dismal conflict,
54 Till that Bellona's bridegroom, lapped in proof,
55 Confronted him with self-comparisons,
56 Point against point, rebellious arm 'gainst arm,
Curbing his lavish spirit; and to conclude,
The victory fell on us.
KING DUNCAN   Great happiness!
ROSS
That now
60 Sweno, the Norways' king, craves composition;
Nor would we deign him burial of his men
62 Till he disbursèd, at Saint Colme's Inch,
63 Ten thousand dollars to our general use.
KING DUNCAN
No more that Thane of Cawdor shall deceive
65 Our bosom interest. Go pronounce his present death
And with his former title greet Macbeth.
ROSS
I'll see it done.
KING DUNCAN
What he hath lost noble Macbeth hath won.   *Exeunt.*

*

---

51 *Norway* the King of Norway   53 *dismal* ominous   54 *Bellona* goddess of
war; *lapped in proof* (1) protected by experience, (2) wearing proven armor
55 *self-comparisons* power comparable with his own   56 *Point* sword   60
composition terms of surrender   62 *Saint Colme's Inch* Inchcolm, an island
near Edinburgh (Inch means "island")   63 *dollars* (the German thaler was a
pan-European silver currency)   65 *bosom interest* heart's trust; *present* imme-
diate

❧ **I.3** *Thunder. Enter the three Witches.*

FIRST WITCH   Where hast thou been, sister?
SECOND WITCH   Killing swine.
THIRD WITCH   Sister, where thou?
FIRST WITCH
  A sailor's wife had chestnuts in her lap
  And munched and munched and munched. "Give
    me," quoth I.
  "Aroint thee, witch!" the rump-fed runnion cries.   6
  Her husband's to Aleppo gone, master o' th' *Tiger:*   7
  But in a sieve I'll thither sail
  And, like a rat without a tail,
  I'll do, I'll do, and I'll do.   10
SECOND WITCH   I'll give thee a wind.
FIRST WITCH   Thou'rt kind.
THIRD WITCH   And I another.
FIRST WITCH
  I myself have all the other,
  And the very ports they blow,   15
  All the quarters that they know
  I' th' shipman's card.   17
  I'll drain him dry as hay.
  Sleep shall neither night nor day
  Hang upon his penthouse lid.   20
  He shall live a man forbid.   21
  Weary sev'nights, nine times nine,
  Shall he dwindle, peak, and pine.   23
  Though his bark cannot be lost,
  Yet it shall be tempest-tossed.
  Look what I have.

I.3 A heath **6** *Aroint thee* get thee gone; *rump-fed runnion* fat-rumped slut
7 *master* captain; *Tiger* (name of his ship) **15** *ports they blow* safe havens
they afflict with storms **17** *shipman's card* nautical chart **20** *penthouse lid*
eyelid (what overhangs the eye) **21** *forbid* accursed **23** *peak* waste away

SECOND WITCH   Show me, show me.

FIRST WITCH
Here I have a pilot's thumb,
Wrecked as homeward he did come.
Drum within.

THIRD WITCH
30   A drum, a drum;
Macbeth doth come.

ALL
32   The weïrd sisters, hand in hand,
33   Posters of the sea and land,
Thus do go about, about,
Thrice to thine, and thrice to mine,
And thrice again, to make up nine.
Peace, the charm's wound up.
Enter Macbeth and Banquo.

MACBETH
So foul and fair a day I have not seen.

BANQUO
39   How far is't called to Forres? What are these,
40   So withered and so wild in their attire
That look not like th' inhabitants o' th' earth
And yet are on't? Live you, or are you aught
That man may question? You seem to understand me,
44   By each at once her choppy finger laying
Upon her skinny lips. You should be women,
And yet your beards forbid me to interpret
That you are so.

MACBETH   Speak, if you can. What are you?

FIRST WITCH
48   All hail, Macbeth! Hail to thee, Thane of Glamis!

---

32 *weïrd* (two syllables: from Old English "wyrd," "fate," hence "supernatural," associated with fate, with an overtone of the uncanny, suggested by F's spelling "weyward")   **33** *Posters* swift travelers   **39** *is't called* do they say it is   **44** *choppy* chapped   **48** *Glamis* (one syllable)

SECOND WITCH
  All hail, Macbeth! Hail to thee, Thane of Cawdor!
THIRD WITCH
  All hail, Macbeth, that shalt be king hereafter!   50
BANQUO
  Good sir, why do you start and seem to fear
  Things that do sound so fair? *[To the Witches]* I' th'
    name of truth,
  Are ye fantastical, or that indeed   53
  Which outwardly ye show? My noble partner
  You greet with present grace and great prediction   55
  Of noble having and of royal hope,
  That he seems rapt withal. To me you speak not.   57
  If you can look into the seeds of time   58
  And say which grain will grow and which will not,
  Speak then to me, who neither beg nor fear   60
  Your favors nor your hate.
FIRST WITCH   Hail!
SECOND WITCH   Hail!
THIRD WITCH   Hail!
FIRST WITCH
  Lesser than Macbeth, and greater.
SECOND WITCH
  Not so happy, yet much happier.   66
THIRD WITCH
  Thou shalt get kings, though thou be none.   67
  So all hail, Macbeth and Banquo!
FIRST WITCH
  Banquo and Macbeth, all hail!
MACBETH
  Stay, you imperfect speakers, tell me more: 70
  By Finel's death I know I am Thane of Glamis,   71

---

53 *fantastical* imaginary, hallucinations 55 *grace* honor 57 *rapt withal*
spellbound at the thought 58 *seeds of time* sources of future events 66
happy fortunate 67 *get* beget 70 *imperfect* incomplete 71 *Finel* or Finley,
Macbeth's father (see textual note)

But how of Cawdor? The Thane of Cawdor lives,
A prosperous gentleman; and to be king
Stands not within the prospect of belief,
No more than to be Cawdor. Say from whence
You owe this strange intelligence, or why
Upon this blasted heath you stop our way
With such prophetic greeting. Speak, I charge you.

Witches vanish.

BANQUO
The earth hath bubbles as the water has,
80   And these are of them. Whither are they vanished?
MACBETH
81   Into the air, and what seemed corporal melted
As breath into the wind. Would they had stayed!
BANQUO
Were such things here as we do speak about?
84   Or have we eaten on the insane root
That takes the reason prisoner?
MACBETH
Your children shall be kings.
BANQUO   You shall be king.
MACBETH
And Thane of Cawdor too. Went it not so?
BANQUO
To th' selfsame tune and words. Who's here?

Enter Ross and Angus.

ROSS
The king hath happily received, Macbeth,
90   The news of thy success; and when he reads
Thy personal venture in the rebels' fight,
92   His wonders and his praises do contend
Which should be thine or his. Silenced with that,
In viewing o'er the rest o' th' selfsame day,

---

81 *corporal* corporeal   **84** *insane* inducing insanity   **90** *reads* considers   **92–93** *His wonders . . . or his* i.e., dumbstruck admiration makes him keep your praises to himself

He finds thee in the stout Norwegian ranks,
Nothing afeard of what thyself didst make,
Strange images of death. As thick as tale   97
Came post with post, and everyone did bear   98
Thy praises in his kingdom's great defense
And poured them down before him.   *100*
ANGUS   We are sent
To give thee from our royal master thanks;
Only to herald thee into his sight,
Not pay thee.
ROSS
And for an earnest of a greater honor,
He bade me, from him, call thee Thane of Cawdor;
In which addition, hail, most worthy thane,   106
For it is thine.
BANQUO   What, can the devil speak true?
MACBETH
The Thane of Cawdor lives. Why do you dress me
In borrowed robes?
ANGUS   Who was the thane lives yet,
But under heavy judgment bears that life   *110*
Which he deserves to lose. Whether he was combined   111
With those of Norway, or did line the rebel   112
With hidden help and vantage, or that with both   113
He labored in his country's wrack, I know not;
But treasons capital, confessed and proved,
Have overthrown him.
MACBETH   *[Aside]*   Glamis, and Thane of Cawdor –
The greatest is behind.   117
     [To Ross and Angus] Thanks for your pains.
     [Aside to Banquo]
Do you not hope your children shall be kings,
When those that gave the Thane of Cawdor to me

---

97 *thick as tale* as fast as they can be counted **98** *post with post* messenger
after messenger **106** *addition* title **111** *combined* leagued **112** *line* support **113** *vantage* assistance **117** *behind* still to come

120 Promised no less to them?

 BANQUO *[To Macbeth]* That, trusted home,
  Might yet enkindle you unto the crown,
  Besides the Thane of Cawdor. But 'tis strange;
  And oftentimes, to win us to our harm,
  The instruments of darkness tell us truths,
  Win us with honest trifles, to betray's
126 In deepest consequence. –
127 Cousins, a word, I pray you.

 MACBETH *[Aside]*   Two truths are told,
128 As happy prologues to the swelling act
  Of the imperial theme. – I thank you, gentlemen. –
  [Aside]
130 This supernatural soliciting
  Cannot be ill, cannot be good. If ill,
  Why hath it given me earnest of success
  Commencing in a truth? I am Thane of Cawdor.
  If good, why do I yield to that suggestion
  Whose horrid image doth unfix my hair
136 And make my seated heart knock at my ribs
137 Against the use of nature? Present fears
  Are less than horrible imaginings:
139 My thought, whose murder yet is but fantastical,
140 Shakes so my single state of man that function
  Is smothered in surmise and nothing is
  But what is not.

 BANQUO   Look how our partner's rapt.

 MACBETH *[Aside]*
  If chance will have me king, why, chance may crown
   me
  Without my stir.

---

120 *home* all the way 126 *deepest consequence* the crucial sequel 127 *Cousins* i.e., fellow lords 128 *swelling act* developing drama 136 *seated* fixed 137 *use* normal habit 139 *fantastical* imaginary 140 *single state of man* both undivided and weak human condition; *function* the power to act

BANQUO   New honors come upon him,
   Like our strange garments, cleave not to their mold   145
   But with the aid of use.
MACBETH   *[Aside]*   Come what come may,
   Time and the hour runs through the roughest day.   147
BANQUO
   Worthy Macbeth, we stay upon your leisure.
MACBETH
   Give me your favor. My dull brain was wrought   149
   With things forgotten. Kind gentlemen, your pains   *150*
   Are registered where every day I turn
   The leaf to read them. Let us toward the king.
      [Aside to Banquo]
   Think upon what hath chanced, and at more time,
   The interim having weighed it, let us speak
   Our free hearts each to other.   155
BANQUO   Very gladly.
MACBETH
   Till then, enough. – Come, friends.   *Exeunt.*
                          *

∾ **I.4** *Flourish. Enter King [Duncan], Lennox,*
       Malcolm, Donalbain, and Attendants.

KING DUNCAN
   Is execution done on Cawdor? Are not
   Those in commission yet returned?   2
MALCOLM   My liege,
   They are not yet come back. But I have spoke
   With one that saw him die, who did report
   That very frankly he confessed his treasons,

---

145 *strange* new   147 *Time . . . day* i.e., the worst day comes to an end
149 *favor* pardon   155 *free hearts* thoughts freely
   I.4 Duncan's camp   2 *in commission* commissioned to carry out the execution

Implored your highness' pardon, and set forth
A deep repentance. Nothing in his life
Became him like the leaving it. He died
9   As one that had been studied in his death
10   To throw away the dearest thing he owed
As 'twere a careless trifle.
KING DUNCAN   There's no art
To find the mind's construction in the face.
He was a gentleman on whom I built
An absolute trust.
      Enter Macbeth, Banquo, Ross, and Angus.
      [To Macbeth]   O worthiest cousin,
The sin of my ingratitude even now
16   Was heavy on me. Thou art so far before
That swiftest wing of recompense is slow
To overtake thee. Would thou hadst less deserved,
19   That the proportion both of thanks and payment
20   Might have been mine. Only I have left to say,
More is thy due than more than all can pay.
MACBETH
The service and the loyalty I owe,
In doing it pays itself. Your highness' part
Is to receive our duties, and our duties
Are to your throne and state children and servants,
Which do but what they should by doing everything
27   Safe toward your love and honor.
KING DUNCAN   Welcome hither.
28   I have begun to plant thee and will labor
To make thee full of growing. Noble Banquo,
30   That hast no less deserved nor must be known
No less to have done so, let me enfold thee
And hold thee to my heart.
BANQUO   There if I grow,

---

9 *studied* rehearsed   **10** *owed* owned   **16** *before* ahead in deserving   **19** *pro-portion* satisfactory apportioning   **27** *Safe* fitting   **28** *plant* nurture

The harvest is your own.

KING DUNCAN   My plenteous joys,
Wanton in fullness, seek to hide themselves   34
In drops of sorrow. Sons, kinsmen, thanes,
And you whose places are the nearest, know
We will establish our estate upon
Our eldest, Malcolm, whom we name hereafter
The Prince of Cumberland; which honor must   39
Not unaccompanied invest him only,   40
But signs of nobleness, like stars, shall shine
On all deservers. From hence to Inverness,
And bind us further to you.

MACBETH
The rest is labor which is not used for you.
I'll be myself the harbinger, and make joyful
The hearing of my wife with your approach;
So, humbly take my leave.

KING DUNCAN   My worthy Cawdor!

MACBETH   [Aside]
The Prince of Cumberland – that is a step
On which I must fall down or else o'erleap,
For in my way it lies. Stars, hide your fires;   50
Let not light see my black and deep desires.
The eye wink at the hand; yet let that be   52
Which the eye fears, when it is done, to see.   Exit.

KING DUNCAN
True, worthy Banquo: he is full so valiant,
And in his commendations I am fed;
It is a banquet to me. Let's after him,
Whose care is gone before to bid us welcome.
It is a peerless kinsman.   Flourish. Exeunt.

                              *

---

34 *Wanton* unrestrained   39 *Prince of Cumberland* (equivalent to the English Prince of Wales, the designated heir to the throne)   52 *wink at the
hand* disregard what the hand does

∽ **I.5** *Enter Macbeth's Wife, alone, with a letter.*

LADY MACBETH   *[Reads.]* "They met me in the day of
2   success; and I have learned by the perfect'st report they
have more in them than mortal knowledge. When I
burned in desire to question them further, they made
themselves air, into which they vanished. Whiles I
6   stood rapt in the wonder of it, came missives from the
king, who all-hailed me Thane of Cawdor, by which
title, before, these weïrd sisters saluted me, and referred
me to the coming on of time with 'Hail, king that shalt
10   be!' This have I thought good to deliver thee, my dearest partner of greatness, that thou mightst not lose the
dues of rejoicing by being ignorant of what greatness is
promised thee. Lay it to thy heart, and farewell."

Glamis thou art, and Cawdor, and shalt be
What thou art promised. Yet do I fear thy nature.
It is too full o' th' milk of human kindness
17   To catch the nearest way. Thou wouldst be great,
Art not without ambition, but without
19   The illness should attend it. What thou wouldst highly,
20   That wouldst thou holily; wouldst not play false,
And yet wouldst wrongly win. Thou'dst have, great
   Glamis,
That which cries "Thus thou must do" if thou have it;
And that which rather thou dost fear to do
Than wishest should be undone. Hie thee hither,
That I may pour my spirits in thine ear
And chastise with the valor of my tongue
27   All that impedes thee from the golden round
28   Which fate and metaphysical aid doth seem

I.5 Within Macbeth's castle at Inverness   **2** *perfect'st report* most reliable evidence   **6** *missives* messengers   **17** *catch . . . way* take the most direct route
19 *illness* wickedness   **27** *round* crown   **28** *metaphysical* supernatural

To have thee crowned withal.   29
   Enter Messenger.   What is your tidings?

MESSENGER
The king comes here tonight.   30

LADY MACBETH   Thou'rt mad to say it!
Is not thy master with him? who, were't so,
Would have informed for preparation.

MESSENGER
So please you, it is true. Our thane is coming.
One of my fellows had the speed of him,
Who, almost dead for breath, had scarcely more   35
Than would make up his message.

LADY MACBETH   Give him tending;
He brings great news.   *Exit Messenger.*
                  The raven himself is hoarse
That croaks the fatal entrance of Duncan
Under my battlements. Come, you spirits
That tend on mortal thoughts, unsex me here,   40
And fill me from the crown to the toe topful
Of direst cruelty. Make thick my blood;
Stop up th' access and passage to remorse,   43
That no compunctious visitings of nature   44
Shake my fell purpose nor keep peace between   45
Th' effect and it. Come to my woman's breasts
And take my milk for gall, you murd'ring ministers,   47
Wherever in your sightless substances   48
You wait on nature's mischief. Come, thick night,   49
And pall thee in the dunnest smoke of hell,   50
That my keen knife see not the wound it makes,
Nor heaven peep through the blanket of the dark
To cry "Hold, hold."
   Enter Macbeth.   Great Glamis, worthy Cawdor,

---

29 *withal* with 35 *breath* want of breath 40 *mortal* deadly 43 *remorse*
pity 44 *nature* natural feeling 45 *fell* fierce 45–46 *keep peace . . . and it*
i.e., lull it from achieving its end 47 *take . . . gall* exchange my milk for gall;
ministers agents 48 *sightless* invisible 49 *wait on* aid 50 *pall thee* shroud
thyself; *dunnest* darkest

Greater than both, by the all-hail hereafter,
Thy letters have transported me beyond
56 This ignorant present, and I feel now
The future in the instant.

MACBETH   My dearest love,
Duncan comes here tonight.

LADY MACBETH   And when goes hence?

MACBETH
Tomorrow, as he purposes.

LADY MACBETH   O, never
60 Shall sun that morrow see.
Your face, my thane, is as a book where men
62 May read strange matters. To beguile the time,
63 Look like the time; bear welcome in your eye,
Your hand, your tongue; look like th' innocent flower,
But be the serpent under't. He that's coming
Must be provided for; and you shall put
67 This night's great business into my dispatch,
Which shall to all our nights and days to come
Give solely sovereign sway and masterdom.

MACBETH
70 We will speak further.

LADY MACBETH   Only look up clear.
71 To alter favor ever is to fear.
Leave all the rest to me.   *Exeunt.*

*

---

56 *ignorant* unaware   62 *beguile* deceive   63 *Look . . . time* act as the occasion requires   67 *dispatch* efficient management   70 *look up clear* appear
untroubled   71 *alter favor* change your countenance

↜ **I.6** *Hautboys and torches. Enter King [Duncan],*
Malcolm, Donalbain, Banquo, Lennox, Macduff,
Ross, Angus, and Attendants.

KING DUNCAN
This castle hath a pleasant seat. The air   1
Nimbly and sweetly recommends itself
Unto our gentle senses.   3
BANQUO   This guest of summer,
The temple-haunting martlet, does approve   4
By his loved mansionry that the heaven's breath   5
Smells wooingly here. No jutty, frieze,   6
Buttress, nor coign of vantage, but this bird   7
Hath made his pendent bed and procreant cradle.   8
Where they most breed and haunt, I have observed
The air is delicate.   10
    Enter Lady [Macbeth].

KING DUNCAN
See, see, our honored hostess!
The love that follows us sometime is our trouble,   12
Which still we thank as love. Herein I teach you
How you shall bid God 'ield us for your pains   14
And thank us for your trouble.
LADY MACBETH   All our service
In every point twice done, and then done double,
Were poor and single business to contend   17
Against those honors deep and broad wherewith
Your majesty loads our house. For those of old,
And the late dignities heaped up to them,   20

I.6 Before Inverness Castle **s.d.** *Hautboys* treble shawms (ancestors of the
modern oboe) 1 *seat* site 3 *gentle* soothed 4 *temple-haunting* nesting
around churches; *martlet* swallow, house martin; *approve* demonstrate 5
loved mansionry beloved nest 6 *jutty* projection 7 *coign of vantage* conve-
nient corner 8 *procreant cradle* cradle for breeding 12–13 *The love ... as*
love our subjects' love sometimes inconveniences us, but we still acknowledge
it as love 14 *God 'ield us* God reward me 17 *single business* simple effort
20 *late* recent

21   We rest your hermits.
KING DUNCAN   Where's the Thane of Cawdor?
22   We coursed him at the heels and had a purpose
     To be his purveyor; but he rides well,
24   And his great love, sharp as his spur, hath holp him
     To his home before us. Fair and noble hostess,
     We are your guest tonight.
LADY MACBETH   Your servants ever
27   Have theirs, themselves, and what is theirs, in count,
     To make their audit at your highness' pleasure,
29   Still to return your own.
KING DUNCAN   Give me your hand.
30   Conduct me to mine host; we love him highly
     And shall continue our graces towards him.
     By your leave, hostess.   *Exeunt.*

✳

∾ **1.7** *Hautboys. Torches. Enter a Sewer, and divers Servants with dishes and service over the stage. Then enter Macbeth.*

MACBETH
1   If it were done when 'tis done, then 'twere well
     It were done quickly. If th' assassination
3   Could trammel up the consequence, and catch
4   With his surcease success, that but this blow
     Might be the be-all and the end-all – here,
6   But here upon this bank and shoal of time,

---

21 *hermits* beadsmen (who are obligated to pray for a benefactor's welfare)
22–23 *had . . . purveyor* (the purveyor was the chief logistical officer in the royal household, arranging for lodging and supplies; Duncan had wished to provide this service for Macbeth)   24 *holp* helped   27 *Have theirs* have their servants; *what is theirs* their possessions; *in count* in trust   29 *Still* always

    I.7 A room off the great hall in Macbeth's castle **s.d.** *Sewer* chief waiter   **1** *done when 'tis done* over and done with when the act is performed   3 *trammel . . . consequence* entrap the consequences as in a net   4 *his surcease* Duncan's death   6 *bank and shoal* sandbank and shallows

We'd jump the life to come. But in these cases　　　7
We still have judgment here, that we but teach　　　8
Bloody instructions, which, being taught, return　　　9
To plague th' inventor. This evenhanded justice　　　10
Commends th' ingredience of our poisoned chalice　　　11
To our own lips. He's here in double trust:
First, as I am his kinsman and his subject,
Strong both against the deed; then, as his host,
Who should against his murderer shut the door,
Not bear the knife myself. Besides, this Duncan
Hath borne his faculties so meek, hath been　　　17
So clear in his great office, that his virtues　　　18
Will plead like angels, trumpet-tongued against
The deep damnation of his taking-off;　　　20
And pity, like a naked newborn babe
Striding the blast, or heaven's cherubin horsed
Upon the sightless couriers of the air,　　　23
Shall blow the horrid deed in every eye
That tears shall drown the wind. I have no spur　　　25
To prick the sides of my intent, but only
Vaulting ambition, which o'erleaps itself
And falls on th' other –
　　　Enter Lady [Macbeth].
　　　　　　　　　　　How now? What news?
LADY MACBETH
He has almost supped. Why have you left the chamber?
MACBETH
Hath he asked for me?　　　30
LADY MACBETH　　　Know you not he has?
MACBETH
We will proceed no further in this business.
He hath honored me of late, and I have bought　　　32

---

7 *jump* risk　8 *that* because　9 *instructions* lessons　10 *evenhanded* impartial
11 *ingredience* contents (the ingredients collectively)　17 *faculties* power　18
clear innocent　23 *sightless couriers* invisible messengers (the winds)　25
That so that　32 *bought* acquired

Golden opinions from all sorts of people,
Which would be worn now in their newest gloss,
Not cast aside so soon.

LADY MACBETH   Was the hope drunk
Wherein you dressed yourself? Hath it slept since?
37 And wakes it now to look so green and pale
At what it did so freely? From this time
Such I account thy love. Art thou afeard
40 To be the same in thine own act and valor
As thou art in desire? Wouldst thou have that
Which thou esteem'st the ornament of life,
And live a coward in thine own esteem,
44 Letting "I dare not" wait upon "I would,"
45 Like the poor cat i' th' adage?

MACBETH   Prithee peace.
I dare do all that may become a man;
47 Who dares do more is none.

LADY MACBETH   What beast was't then
48 That made you break this enterprise to me?
When you durst do it, then you were a man;
50 And to be more than what you were, you would
Be so much more the man. Nor time nor place
52 Did then adhere, and yet you would make both.
53 They have made themselves, and that their fitness now
Does unmake you. I have given suck, and know
How tender 'tis to love the babe that milks me:
I would, while it was smiling in my face,
Have plucked my nipple from his boneless gums
And dashed the brains out, had I so sworn as you
59 Have done to this.

MACBETH   If we should fail?

---

37 *green* bilious 44 *wait upon* preempt 45 *cat i' th' adage* (the adage says,
"The cat would eat fish but will not wet her feet") 47 *none* not a man 48
break broach 52 *adhere* agree 53 *that their fitness* their very fitness 59
fail? . . . fail? (F's punctuation mark could represent both modern ? and !; it
is thus not clear whether Lady Macbeth is acknowledging the possibility of
failure)

LADY MACBETH   We fail?   60
  But screw your courage to the sticking place
  And we'll not fail. When Duncan is asleep,   62
  Whereto the rather shall his day's hard journey
  Soundly invite him, his two chamberlains   64
  Will I with wine and wassail so convince   65
  That memory, the warder of the brain,   66
  Shall be a fume, and the receipt of reason   67
  A limbeck only. When in swinish sleep
  Their drenchèd natures lies as in a death,
  What cannot you and I perform upon   70
  Th' unguarded Duncan? what not put upon
  His spongy officers, who shall bear the guilt   72
  Of our great quell?
MACBETH   Bring forth men-children only;   73
  For thy undaunted mettle should compose
  Nothing but males. Will it not be received,
  When we have marked with blood those sleepy two
  Of his own chamber and used their very daggers,   77
  That they have done't?
LADY MACBETH   Who dares receive it other,
  As we shall make our griefs and clamor roar
  Upon his death?
MACBETH   I am settled, and bend up   80
  Each corporal agent to this terrible feat.   81
  Away, and mock the time with fairest show;
  False face must hide what the false heart doth know.
                                  Exeunt.

*

---

60 *But* (1) however, (2) merely; *sticking place* (the notch holding the string taut, on either a crossbow or a musical instrument)   **62** *the rather* the sooner   **64** *wassail* liquor; *convince* overwhelm   **65** *warder* guardian   **66** *fume* vapor; *receipt* receptacle   **67** *limbeck* distilling device   **72** *quell* killing   **73** *mettle* valor   **77** *other* otherwise   **81** *mock* delude

∾ **II.1** *Enter Banquo, and Fleance, with a torch before him.*

BANQUO
  How goes the night, boy?
FLEANCE
  The moon is down; I have not heard the clock.
BANQUO
  And she goes down at twelve.
FLEANCE
  I take't, 'tis later, sir.
BANQUO
5 Hold, take my sword. There's husbandry in heaven;
  Their candles are all out. Take thee that too.
7 A heavy summons lies like lead upon me,
  And yet I would not sleep. Merciful powers,
  Restrain in me the cursèd thoughts that nature
10 Gives way to in repose.
     Enter Macbeth, and a Servant with a torch.
                       Give me my sword!
  Who's there?
MACBETH
  A friend.
BANQUO
  What, sir, not yet at rest? The king's abed.
  He hath been in unusual pleasure and
15 Sent forth great largess to your offices.
  This diamond he greets your wife withal
17 By the name of most kind hostess, and shut up
  In measureless content.
MACBETH   Being unprepared,
19 Our will became the servant to defect,

II.1 Another room in Macbeth's castle **5** *husbandry* economy **7** *summons* signal to sleep **15** *largess . . . offices* gifts to your household staff **17** *shut up* concluded **19** *will* good will; *defect* deficient means

Which else should free have wrought.   20

BANQUO   All's well.
I dreamt last night of the three weïrd sisters.
To you they have showed some truth.

MACBETH   I think not of them.
Yet when we can entreat an hour to serve,
We would spend it in some words upon that business,
If you would grant the time.

BANQUO   At your kind'st leisure.

MACBETH
If you shall cleave to my consent, when 'tis,   26
It shall make honor for you.

BANQUO   So I lose none
In seeking to augment it, but still keep
My bosom franchised and allegiance clear,   29
I shall be counseled.   30

MACBETH   Good repose the while.

BANQUO
Thanks, sir. The like to you.

                          Exeunt Banquo [and Fleance].

MACBETH   *[To Servant]*
Go bid thy mistress, when my drink is ready,
She strike upon the bell. Get thee to bed. *Exit [Servant].*
Is this a dagger which I see before me,
The handle toward my hand? Come, let me clutch thee.
I have thee not, and yet I see thee still.
Art thou not, fatal vision, sensible
To feeling as to sight? or art thou but
A dagger of the mind, a false creation
Proceeding from the heat-oppressèd brain?   40
I see thee yet, in form as palpable
As this which now I draw.

---

20 *should . . . wrought* would have worked liberally   26 *cleave . . . 'tis* support my interests at the proper time   29 *franchised* free of obligations   30 *be counseled* take your advice   40 *heat-oppressèd* overheated

Thou marshal'st me the way that I was going,
And such an instrument I was to use.
45 Mine eyes are made the fools o' th' other senses,
Or else worth all the rest. I see thee still,
47 And on thy blade and dudgeon gouts of blood,
Which was not so before. There's no such thing.
49 It is the bloody business which informs
50 Thus to mine eyes. Now o'er the one half-world
Nature seems dead, and wicked dreams abuse
The curtained sleep. Witchcraft celebrates
53 Pale Hecate's offerings; and withered murder,
54 Alarumed by his sentinel, the wolf,
Whose howl's his watch, thus with his stealthy pace,
56 With Tarquin's ravishing side, towards his design
Moves like a ghost. Thou sure and firm-set earth,
Hear not my steps which way they walk, for fear
Thy very stones prate of my whereabout
60 And take the present horror from the time,
Which now suits with it. Whiles I threat, he lives;
Words to the heat of deeds too cold breath gives.
    A bell rings.
I go, and it is done. The bell invites me.
Hear it not, Duncan, for it is a knell
That summons thee to heaven, or to hell.   *Exit.*

*

45 *made the fools o'* playing tricks on   47 *dudgeon* handle; *gouts* spots   49 *informs* (1) reports, (2) takes shape   53 *Hecate's offerings* worship of Hecate, goddess of the moon and of witchcraft   54 *Alarumed* given the signal   56 *Tarquin* Sextus Tarquinius, the ancient Roman king who raped the chaste Lucretia (the story is recounted in Shakespeare's poem *The Rape of Lucrece*); *side* arrogance (see textual notes)   60 *take . . . time* i.e., break the silence and thus disrupt the horror appropriate to the moment

∾ **II.2** *Enter Lady [Macbeth].*

LADY MACBETH
>   That which hath made them drunk hath made me bold;
>   What hath quenched them hath given me fire. *[An owl*
>   *shrieks.]* Hark! Peace.
>   It was the owl that shrieked, the fatal bellman   3
>   Which gives the stern'st good-night. He is about it.
>   The doors are open, and the surfeited grooms
>   Do mock their charge with snores. I have drugged their   6
>   possets,
>   That death and nature do contend about them   7
>   Whether they live or die.

MACBETH   *[Within]*   Who's there? What, ho?

LADY MACBETH
>   Alack, I am afraid they have awaked,
>   And 'tis not done. Th' attempt, and not the deed,   10
>   Confounds us. Hark! I laid their daggers ready –   11
>   He could not miss 'em. Had he not resembled
>   My father as he slept, I had done't.
>   *Enter Macbeth [with two bloody daggers].*   My husband!

MACBETH
>   I have done the deed. Didst thou not hear a noise?

LADY MACBETH
>   I heard the owl scream and the crickets cry.
>   Did not you speak?

MACBETH   When?

LADY MACBETH   Now.

MACBETH   As I descended?

LADY MACBETH   Ay.   20

MACBETH   Hark! Who lies i' th' second chamber?

LADY MACBETH   Donalbain.

MACBETH   This is a sorry sight.

II.2 **3** *bellman* night watchman   **6** *possets* warm milk with spices and liquor
7 *That* so that   **11** *Confounds* defeats

LADY MACBETH
    A foolish thought to say a sorry sight.

MACBETH
    There's one did laugh in's sleep, and one cried "Murder!"
26   That they did wake each other. I stood and heard them.
27   But they did say their prayers and addressed them
    Again to sleep.

LADY MACBETH   There are two lodged together.

MACBETH
    One cried "God bless us" and "Amen" the other,
30   As they had seen me with these hangman's hands.
    List'ning their fear, I could not say "Amen"
    When they did say "God bless us."

LADY MACBETH   Consider it not so deeply.

MACBETH
    But wherefore could not I pronounce "Amen"?
    I had most need of blessing, and "Amen"
    Stuck in my throat.

LADY MACBETH   These deeds must not be thought
    After these ways; so, it will make us mad.

MACBETH
    Methought I heard a voice cry "Sleep no more!
    Macbeth does murder sleep" – the innocent sleep,
40   Sleep that knits up the raveled sleave of care,
    The death of each day's life, sore labor's bath,
42   Balm of hurt minds, great nature's second course,
    Chief nourisher in life's feast.

LADY MACBETH   What do you mean?

MACBETH
    Still it cried "Sleep no more!" to all the house;
    "Glamis hath murdered sleep, and therefore Cawdor

---

26 *That* so that 27 *addressed them* prepared 30 *As* as if; *hangman's hands*
executioner's hands (hence, bloody) 40 *knits . . . sleave* smoothes the tan-
gled skein 42 *second course* the main, and most satisfying course (sleep, after
labor)

Shall sleep no more, Macbeth shall sleep no more."

LADY MACBETH
Who was it that thus cried? Why, worthy thane,
You do unbend your noble strength to think   48
So brainsickly of things. Go get some water
And wash this filthy witness from your hand.   50
Why did you bring these daggers from the place?
They must lie there: go carry them and smear
The sleepy grooms with blood.

MACBETH   I'll go no more.
I am afraid to think what I have done;
Look on't again I dare not.

LADY MACBETH   Infirm of purpose!
Give me the daggers. The sleeping and the dead
Are but as pictures. 'Tis the eye of childhood
That fears a painted devil. If he do bleed,
I'll gild the faces of the grooms withal,   59
For it must seem their guilt.   *Exit.* 60
     Knock within.

MACBETH   Whence is that knocking?
How is't with me when every noise appalls me?
What hands are here? Ha! they pluck out mine eyes.
Will all great Neptune's ocean wash this blood
Clean from my hand? No, this my hand will rather
The multitudinous seas incarnadine,   65
Making the green one red.   66
     Enter Lady [Macbeth].

LADY MACBETH
My hands are of your color, but I shame
To wear a heart so white.
     Knock.   I hear a knocking
At the south entry. Retire we to our chamber.

---

48 *unbend* slacken   50 *witness* evidence   59 *gild* paint   65 *incarnadine* redden   66 *the green one* Neptune's ocean (l. 63); most editors, following Johnson, take "one" to mean "uniformly," but F has a comma after "one"

70   A little water clears us of this deed.
      How easy is it then! Your constancy
72   Hath left you unattended.
          Knock.   Hark, more knocking.
73   Get on your nightgown, lest occasion call us
74   And show us to be watchers. Be not lost
      So poorly in your thoughts.
MACBETH
      To know my deed, 'twere best not know myself.
          Knock.
      Wake Duncan with thy knocking – I would thou
      couldst.   *Exeunt.*

                        ∗

❧ **II.3** *Enter a Porter. Knocking within.*

PORTER   Here's a knocking indeed. If a man were porter
2   of hell gate, he should have old turning the key.
       (Knock.) Knock, knock, knock. Who's there, i' th' name
4   of Beelzebub? Here's a farmer that hanged himself on th'
5   expectation of plenty. Come in time – have napkins
       enow about you; here you'll sweat for't. *(Knock.)* Knock,
       knock. Who's there, in th' other devil's name? Faith,
8   here's an equivocator, that could swear in both the scales
       against either scale; who committed treason enough for
10   God's sake, yet could not equivocate to heaven. O come
       in, equivocator. *(Knock.)* Knock, knock, knock. Who's
       there? Faith, here's an English tailor come hither for

---

72 *left you unattended* deserted you   73 *nightgown* dressing gown   74
watchers i.e., awake
    II.3   2 *old* too much   4 *Beelzebub* one of the biblical devils   4–5
farmer . . . plenty (because a crop surplus would lower prices and diminish
his profit)   5 *Come in time* you've come at the right time   5–6 *napkins enow*
enough handkerchiefs (to wipe away the sweat caused by hellfire)   8 *equivocator* deceiver, prevaricator (here alluding to the equivocating testimony
given by the Jesuit conspirators in the Gunpowder Plot, 1605)

stealing out of a French hose. Come in, tailor. Here you   13
may roast your goose. *(Knock.)* Knock, knock. Never at   14
quiet! What are you? – But this place is too cold for hell.
I'll devil-porter it no further. I had thought to have let
in some of all professions that go the primrose way to th'
everlasting bonfire. *(Knock.)* Anon, anon! *[Opens the
door.]* I pray you remember the porter.   19
    Enter Macduff and Lennox.

MACDUFF

Was it so late, friend, ere you went to bed,   20
That you do lie so late?

PORTER   Faith, sir, we were carousing till the second   22
cock; and drink, sir, is a great provoker of three things.

MACDUFF   What three things does drink especially pro-
voke?

PORTER   Marry, sir, nose-painting, sleep, and urine.   26
Lechery, sir, it provokes, and unprovokes: it provokes
the desire, but it takes away the performance. Therefore
much drink may be said to be an equivocator with
lechery: it makes him, and it mars him; it sets him on,   30
and it takes him off; it persuades him, and disheartens
him; makes him stand to, and not stand to; in conclu-   32
sion, equivocates him in a sleep, and, giving him the   33
lie, leaves him.

MACDUFF   I believe drink gave thee the lie last night.   35

PORTER   That it did, sir, i' the very throat on me; but I   36
requited him for his lie; and, I think, being too strong

---

13 *stealing . . . hose* (probably skimping on material in the making of French
hose, which were tight-fitting, and hence would lead to discovery)   14 *roast
your goose* heat your iron (a goose is a long-handled tailor's iron)   19 *remember* i.e., tip   22–23 *second cock* second crowing of the cock (i.e., till early
morning)   26 *nose-painting* i.e., a red nose (from habitual drunkenness)
32 *stand to* grow erect   33 *equivocates . . . sleep* i.e., satisfies him only by
putting him to sleep; *giving . . . lie* (1) deceiving him (because he cannot perform sexually), (2) overthrowing him, (3) making him lose his erection, (4)
accusing him of lying   35 *gave thee the lie* (1) made you a liar, (2) made you
fall down   36 *i' the very throat* (to lie in the throat was to lie egregiously)

38   for him, though he took up my legs sometime, yet I
39   made a shift to cast him.
40   MACDUFF   Is thy master stirring?
            Enter Macbeth.
      Our knocking has awaked him: here he comes.
      LENNOX
      Good morrow, noble sir.
      MACBETH   Good morrow, both.
      MACDUFF
      Is the king stirring, worthy thane?
      MACBETH   Not yet.
      MACDUFF
44   He did command me to call timely on him;
45   I have almost slipped the hour.
      MACBETH   I'll bring you to him.
      MACDUFF
      I know this is a joyful trouble to you;
      But yet 'tis one.
      MACBETH
48   The labor we delight in physics pain.
      This is the door.
      MACDUFF   I'll make so bold to call,
50   For 'tis my limited service.   *Exit Macduff.*
      LENNOX
      Goes the king hence today?
      MACBETH   He does – he did appoint so.
      LENNOX
      The night has been unruly. Where we lay,
      Our chimneys were blown down; and, as they say,
      Lamentings heard i' th' air, strange screams of death,
      And prophesying, with accents terrible,
56   Of dire combustion and confused events

---

38 *took up my legs* (1) made me fall down from drunkenness, (2) overthrew
me in wrestling 39 *cast* throw 44 *timely* early 45 *slipped* missed 48
physics pain cures the trouble it gives us 50 *limited* appointed 56 *combustion* tumult

New hatched to th' woeful time. The obscure bird   57
Clamored the livelong night. Some say the earth
Was feverous and did shake.

MACBETH   'Twas a rough night.

LENNOX

My young remembrance cannot parallel   60
A fellow to it.

    Enter Macduff.

MACDUFF

O horror, horror, horror –
Tongue nor heart cannot conceive nor name thee!

MACBETH AND LENNOX   What's the matter?

MACDUFF

Confusion now hath made his masterpiece: 65
Most sacrilegious murder hath broke ope
The Lord's anointed temple and stole thence
The life o' th' building!

MACBETH   What is't you say? the life?

LENNOX

Mean you his majesty?

MACDUFF

Approach the chamber and destroy your sight   70
With a new Gorgon. Do not bid me speak.   71
See, and then speak yourselves.

        Exeunt Macbeth and Lennox.

        Awake, awake!

Ring the alarum bell! Murder and treason!
Banquo and Donalbain! Malcolm, awake!
Shake off this downy sleep, death's counterfeit,
And look on death itself. Up, up, and see
The great doom's image. Malcolm! Banquo!   77
As from your graves rise up and walk like sprites   78

---

57 *obscure bird* i.e., the owl   65 *Confusion* destruction   71 *Gorgon* Medusa,
a mythical monster whose terrible aspect turned those who saw her to stone
77 *great doom* the Last Judgment   78 *sprites* ghosts

79   To countenance this horror.
            Bell rings. Enter Lady [Macbeth].
LADY MACBETH   What's the business,
80   That such a hideous trumpet calls to parley
      The sleepers of the house? Speak, speak!
MACDUFF   O gentle lady,
      'Tis not for you to hear what I can speak:
      The repetition in a woman's ear
      Would murder as it fell.
            Enter Banquo.   O Banquo, Banquo,
      Our royal master's murdered!
LADY MACBETH   Woe, alas –
      What, in our house?
BANQUO   Too cruel anywhere.
      Dear Duff, I prithee contradict thyself
      And say it is not so.
            Enter Macbeth, Lennox, and Ross.
MACBETH
      Had I but died an hour before this chance,
90   I had lived a blessèd time; for from this instant
91   There's nothing serious in mortality:
92   All is but toys. Renown and grace is dead,
93   The wine of life is drawn, and the mere lees
94   Is left this vault to brag of.
            Enter Malcolm and Donalbain.
DONALBAIN
      What is amiss?
MACBETH   You are, and do not know't.
      The spring, the head, the fountain of your blood
      Is stopped, the very source of it is stopped.
MACDUFF
      Your royal father's murdered.
MALCOLM   O, by whom?

---

79 *countenance* appear in keeping with   91 *mortality* human life   92 *toys* trifles   93 *lees* dregs   94 *vault* (1) world (with its *vault* the sky), (2) wine cellar

LENNOX
    Those of his chamber, as it seemed, had done't.
    Their hands and faces were all badged with blood;   100
    So were their daggers, which unwiped we found
    Upon their pillows. They stared and were distracted.
    No man's life was to be trusted with them.

MACBETH
    O, yet I do repent me of my fury
    That I did kill them.

MACDUFF   Wherefore did you so?

MACBETH
    Who can be wise, amazed, temp'rate and furious,
    Loyal and neutral, in a moment? No man.   107
    The expedition of my violent love   108
    Outrun the pauser, reason. Here lay Duncan,
    His silver skin laced with his golden blood;   *110*
    And his gashed stabs looked like a breach in nature
    For ruin's wasteful entrance: there, the murderers,
    Steeped in the colors of their trade, their daggers
    Unmannerly breeched with gore. Who could refrain   114
    That had a heart to love, and in that heart
    Courage to make's love known?

LADY MACBETH   Help me hence, ho!

MACDUFF
    Look to the lady.   117

MALCOLM   *[Aside to Donalbain]*
              Why do we hold our tongues,
    That most may claim this argument for ours?   118

DONALBAIN   *[To Malcolm]*
    What should be spoken here,
    Where our fate, hid in an auger hole,   120
    May rush and seize us? Let's away:

---

100 *badged* marked   107 *Loyal and neutral* loyal to Duncan and impartial
on the question of the grooms' guilt   108 *expedition* haste   114 *Unman-
nerly breeched* indecently garbed   117 *Look to* look after   118 *argument for
ours* matter as chiefly our concern   120 *auger hole* i.e., any tiny cranny

Our tears are not yet brewed.

MALCOLM   *[To Donalbain]*   Nor our strong sorrow
123   Upon the foot of motion.

BANQUO   Look to the lady.
                   [Lady Macbeth is assisted out.]
124   And when we have our naked frailties hid,
That suffer in exposure, let us meet
126   And question this most bloody piece of work,
127   To know it further. Fears and scruples shake us.
In the great hand of God I stand, and thence
129   Against the undivulged pretense I fight
130   Of treasonous malice.

MACDUFF   And so do I.

ALL   So all.

MACBETH
Let's briefly put on manly readiness
And meet i' th' hall together.

ALL   Well contented.
       Exeunt [all but Malcolm and Donalbain].

MALCOLM
What will you do? Let's not consort with them.
To show an unfelt sorrow is an office
Which the false man does easy. I'll to England.

DONALBAIN
To Ireland I. Our separated fortune
Shall keep us both the safer. Where we are
138   There's daggers in men's smiles; the near in blood,
The nearer bloody.

MALCOLM   This murderous shaft that's shot
140   Hath not yet lighted, and our safest way
Is to avoid the aim. Therefore to horse,
142   And let us not be dainty of leave-taking

---

123 *Upon . . . motion* yet in motion   **124** *frailties hid* bodies clothed   **126** *question* discuss   **127** *scruples* doubts   **129** *undivulged pretense* secret purposes   **138** *near* nearer   **138–39** *the near . . . bloody* i.e., the closer we are to Duncan in blood, the more likely we are to be killed   **140** *lighted* landed   **142** *dainty of* scrupulous about

But shift away. There's warrant in that theft   143
Which steals itself when there's no mercy left.   *Exeunt.*

*

❧ **II.4** *Enter Ross with an Old Man.*

OLD MAN
  Threescore and ten I can remember well;   1
  Within the volume of which time I have seen
  Hours dreadful and things strange, but this sore night
  Hath trifled former knowings.   4
ROSS   Ha, good father,
  Thou seest the heavens, as troubled with man's act,   5
  Threatens his bloody stage. By th' clock 'tis day,
  And yet dark night strangles the traveling lamp.   7
  Is't night's predominance, or the day's shame,   8
  That darkness does the face of earth entomb
  When living light should kiss it?   10
OLD MAN   'Tis unnatural,
  Even like the deed that's done. On Tuesday last
  A falcon, tow'ring in her pride of place,   12
  Was by a mousing owl hawked at and killed.   13
ROSS
  And Duncan's horses – a thing most strange and
   certain –
  Beauteous and swift, the minions of their race,   15
  Turned wild in nature, broke their stalls, flung out,   16
  Contending 'gainst obedience, as they would make
  War with mankind.
OLD MAN   'Tis said they ate each other.

---

143 *shift* steal; *warrant* justification
  II.4 Somewhere outside the castle **1** *Threescore and ten* seventy years
4 *trifled . . . knowings* made former experiences seem trifling **5** *as . . . act* as
if troubled by the actions of men **7** *traveling lamp* i.e., the sun **8** *predomi-*
nance powerful influence **12** *tow'ring* soaring **13** *mousing owl* owl that
preys on mice (a mere domestic predator); *hawked at* caught on the wing
15 *minions* favorites (the most highly prized) **16** *flung out* lunged about

ROSS
    They did so, to th' amazement of mine eyes
20 That looked upon't.
            Enter Macduff.   Here comes the good Macduff.
    How goes the world, sir, now?
MACDUFF   Why, see you not?
ROSS
    Is't known who did this more than bloody deed?
MACDUFF
    Those that Macbeth hath slain.
ROSS   Alas the day,
24 What good could they pretend?
MACDUFF   They were suborned.
    Malcolm and Donalbain, the king's two sons,
    Are stol'n away and fled, which puts upon them
    Suspicion of the deed.
ROSS   'Gainst nature still.
28 Thriftless ambition, that will ravin up
29 Thine own life's means! Then 'tis most like
30 The sovereignty will fall upon Macbeth.
MACDUFF
31 He is already named, and gone to Scone
32 To be invested.
ROSS   Where is Duncan's body?
MACDUFF
33 Carried to Colmekill,
    The sacred storehouse of his predecessors
    And guardian of their bones.
ROSS   Will you to Scone?
MACDUFF
    No, cousin, I'll to Fife.
ROSS   Well, I will thither.

---

24 *pretend* expect; *suborned* bribed   28 *Thriftless* wasteful; *ravin up* greedily
devour   29 *like* likely   31 *named* chosen; *Scone* (where Scottish kings tradi-
tionally were crowned; near Perth)   32 *invested* crowned   33 *Colmekill* (the
island of Iona, in the Hebrides, burial place of the ancient Scottish kings)

MACDUFF
    Well, may you see things well done there. Adieu,
    Lest our old robes sit easier than our new.
ROSS
    Farewell, father.
OLD MAN
    God's benison go with you, and with those   40
    That would make good of bad, and friends of foes.

                                        Exeunt omnes.

                            *

∾ **III.1** *Enter Banquo.*

BANQUO
    Thou hast it now – king, Cawdor, Glamis, all,
    As the weïrd women promised; and I fear
    Thou play'dst most foully for't. Yet it was said
    It should not stand in thy posterity,   4
    But that myself should be the root and father
    Of many kings. If there come truth from them –
    As upon thee, Macbeth, their speeches shine –   7
    Why, by the verities on thee made good,
    May they not be my oracles as well
    And set me up in hope? But hush, no more.   10
        Sennet sounded. Enter Macbeth as King, Lady
        [Macbeth as Queen], Lennox, Ross, Lords, and
        Attendants.
MACBETH
    Here's our chief guest.
LADY MACBETH   If he had been forgotten,
    It had been as a gap in our great feast,
    And all-thing unbecoming.   13

---

40 *benison* blessing
    III.1 The royal castle at Forres **4** *stand . . . posterity* continue through
your heirs **7** *shine* look auspicious **10 s.d.** *Sennet* trumpet salute **13** *all-*
thing altogether

MACBETH

14   Tonight we hold a solemn supper, sir,
    And I'll request your presence.

BANQUO   Let your highness
    Command upon me, to the which my duties
    Are with a most indissoluble tie
    Forever knit.

MACBETH   Ride you this afternoon?

BANQUO
    Ay, my good lord.

MACBETH

20   We should have else desired your good advice,
21   Which still hath been both grave and prosperous,
    In this day's council; but we'll take tomorrow.
    Is't far you ride?

BANQUO
    As far, my lord, as will fill up the time
25   'Twixt this and supper. Go not my horse the better,
26   I must become a borrower of the night
    For a dark hour or twain.

MACBETH   Fail not our feast.

BANQUO
    My lord, I will not.

MACBETH
    We hear our bloody cousins are bestowed
30   In England and in Ireland, not confessing
    Their cruel parricide, filling their hearers
32   With strange invention. But of that tomorrow,
33   When therewithal we shall have cause of state
    Craving us jointly. Hie you to horse. Adieu,
    Till you return at night. Goes Fleance with you?

---

14 *solemn supper* formal banquet   **21** *still* always; *prosperous* profitable   **25** *Go . . . better* i.e., unless my horse goes faster than anticipated   **26** *borrower of* i.e., borrower of time from   **32** *invention* falsehoods   **33–34** *cause . . . jointly* state business requiring our joint attention

BANQUO

Ay, my good lord. Our time does call upon's.

MACBETH

I wish your horses swift and sure of foot,
And so I do commend you to their backs.
Farewell.   *Exit Banquo.*
Let every man be master of his time   40
Till seven at night. To make society
The sweeter welcome, we will keep ourself
Till suppertime alone. While then, God be with you.   43
                         Exeunt Lords [and others].

    [To Servant]

Sirrah, a word with you. Attend those men   44
Our pleasure?

SERVANT

They are, my lord, without the palace gate.

MACBETH

Bring them before us.   *Exit Servant.*
To be thus is nothing, but to be safely thus.   48
Our fears in Banquo stick deep,   49
And in his royalty of nature reigns that   50
Which would be feared. 'Tis much he dares;   51
And to that dauntless temper of his mind
He hath a wisdom that doth guide his valor
To act in safety. There is none but he
Whose being I do fear; and under him
My genius is rebuked, as it is said   56
Mark Antony's was by Caesar. He chid the sisters   57
When first they put the name of king upon me,
And bade them speak to him. Then, prophetlike,
They hailed him father to a line of kings.   60
Upon my head they placed a fruitless crown

---

43 *While* until   44 *Sirrah* (form of address to an inferior) 44–45 *Attend . . .
pleasure* are those men awaiting my orders   48 *but* unless   49 *in Banquo*
about Banquo; *stick deep* are deep-seated   50 *royalty of nature* royal nature
51 *would be* deserves to be   56 *genius is rebuked* guiding spirit is daunted
57 *Mark Antony's . . . Caesar* (see *Antony and Cleopatra*, II.3.20–22)

     And put a barren scepter in my grip,
     Thence to be wrenched with an unlineal hand,
     No son of mine succeeding. If't be so,
65   For Banquo's issue have I filed my mind;
     For them the gracious Duncan have I murdered;
67   Put rancors in the vessel of my peace
68   Only for them, and mine eternal jewel
69   Given to the common enemy of man
70   To make them kings – the seeds of Banquo kings.
71   Rather than so, come, Fate, into the list,
72   And champion me to th' utterance. Who's there?
          Enter Servant and two Murderers.
          [To Servant]
     Now go to the door and stay there till we call.
                                        Exit Servant.

     Was it not yesterday we spoke together?
MURDERERS
     It was, so please your highness.
MACBETH   Well then, now
     Have you considered of my speeches? Know
     That it was he, in the times past, which held you
78   So under fortune, which you thought had been
     Our innocent self. This I made good to you
80   In our last conference, passed in probation with you
81   How you were borne in hand, how crossed; the instru-
          ments;
82   Who wrought with them; and all things else that might
83   To half a soul and to a notion crazed
     Say "Thus did Banquo."

---

65 *filed* defiled   67 *rancors* hatreds   68 *eternal jewel* immortal soul   69
common enemy of man i.e., Satan   71 *list* lists (the tournament field where
knights answered challenges)   72 *champion . . . utterance* (1) support me to
the utmost, (2) fight with me to the death; *champion* (1) defend, (2) challenge   78 *under fortune* out of favor with fortune   80 *passed in probation
with* proved to   81 *borne in hand* manipulated, deceived; *crossed* thwarted;
instruments agents   82 *wrought* worked   83 *half a soul* (even) a half-wit; *notion crazed* insane mind

FIRST MURDERER   You made it known to us.
MACBETH
  I did so; and went further, which is now
  Our point of second meeting. Do you find   86
  Your patience so predominant in your nature
  That you can let this go? Are you so gospeled   88
  To pray for this good man and for his issue,
  Whose heavy hand hath bowed you to the grave   90
  And beggared yours forever?   91
FIRST MURDERER   We are men, my liege.
MACBETH
  Ay, in the catalogue ye go for men,   92
  As hounds and greyhounds, mongrels, spaniels, curs,   93
  Shoughs, waterrugs, and demiwolves are clept   94
  All by the name of dogs. The valued file   95
  Distinguishes the swift, the slow, the subtle;
  The housekeeper, the hunter, every one   97
  According to the gift which bounteous nature
  Hath in him closed, whereby he does receive   99
  Particular addition, from the bill   100
  That writes them all alike; and so of men.
  Now, if you have a station in the file,   102
  Not i' th' worst rank of manhood, say't;
  And I will put that business in your bosoms   104
  Whose execution takes your enemy off,   105
  Grapples you to the heart and love of us,
  Who wear our health but sickly in his life,
  Which in his death were perfect.
SECOND MURDERER   I am one, my liege,
  Whom the vile blows and buffets of the world

---

86 *Our point of* the point of our   **88** *gospeled* religious   **91** *yours* your families   **92** *catalogue* inventory, classification   **93** *curs* watchdogs or sheep dogs
94 *shoughs* lapdogs; *waterrugs* long-haired water dogs; *clept* called   **95** *valued*
file list of valued qualities   **97** *housekeeper* watchdog   **99** *closed* incorporated
100 *addition . . . bill* distinction, contrary to the catalogue   **102** *station . . .*
file place on the list   **104** *bosoms* trust   **105** *execution . . . off* accomplish-
ment kills your enemy

110   Have so incensed that I am reckless what
       I do to spite the world.
FIRST MURDERER   And I another,
       So weary with disasters, tugged with fortune,
113   That I would set my life on any chance
114   To mend it or be rid on't.
MACBETH   Both of you
       Know Banquo was your enemy.
MURDERERS   True, my lord.
MACBETH
116   So is he mine, and in such bloody distance
       That every minute of his being thrusts
118   Against my near'st of life; and though I could
       With barefaced power sweep him from my sight
120   And bid my will avouch it, yet I must not,
121   For certain friends that are both his and mine,
122   Whose loves I may not drop, but wail his fall
       Who I myself struck down. And thence it is
       That I to your assistance do make love,
       Masking the business from the common eye
       For sundry weighty reasons.
SECOND MURDERER   We shall, my lord,
       Perform what you command us.
FIRST MURDERER   Though our lives —
MACBETH
       Your spirits shine through you. Within this hour at
          most
       I will advise you where to plant yourselves,
130   Acquaint you with the perfect spy o' th' time
       The moment on't, for't must be done tonight
132   And something from the palace — always thought

_____

113 *set* risk 114 *on't* of it 116 *distance* enmity 118 *near'st of life* vital
parts 120 *avouch* justify 121 *For* because of 122 *wail* I must bewail
130 *Acquaint . . . time* (a famous crux: the general sense is "spy out the perfect time and inform you of it," but the syntax has not been satisfactorily explained) 132 *something* some distance; *thought* bearing in mind

That I require a clearness; and with him,   133
To leave no rubs nor botches in the work,   134
Fleance his son, that keeps him company,
Whose absence is no less material to me
Than is his father's, must embrace the fate
Of that dark hour. Resolve yourselves apart;
I'll come to you anon.
MURDERERS   We are resolved, my lord.
MACBETH
I'll call upon you straight. Abide within.   140
It is concluded. Banquo, thy soul's flight,
If it find heaven, must find it out tonight.   *Exeunt.*

                            ∗

∾ **III.2** *Enter Macbeth's Lady and a Servant.*

LADY MACBETH
Is Banquo gone from court?
SERVANT
Ay, madam, but returns again tonight.
LADY MACBETH
Say to the king I would attend his leisure
For a few words.
SERVANT   Madam, I will.   *Exit.*
LADY MACBETH
Naught's had, all's spent,
Where our desire is got without content.
'Tis safer to be that which we destroy
Than by destruction dwell in doubtful joy.
    Enter Macbeth.
How now, my lord? Why do you keep alone,
Of sorriest fancies your companions making,   10

---

133 *clearness* alibi 134 *rubs nor botches* problems or flaws
    III.2 A private chamber in the castle 10 *sorriest fancies* most painful
delusions

Using those thoughts which should indeed have died
12   With them they think on? Things without all remedy
Should be without regard. What's done is done.

MACBETH

14   We have scorched the snake, not killed it.
15   She'll close and be herself, whilst our poor malice
Remains in danger of her former tooth.
17   But let the frame of things disjoint, both the worlds
     suffer,
Ere we will eat our meal in fear, and sleep
In the affliction of these terrible dreams
20   That shake us nightly. Better be with the dead,
Whom we, to gain our peace, have sent to peace,
22   Than on the torture of the mind to lie
23   In restless ecstasy. Duncan is in his grave;
After life's fitful fever he sleeps well.
Treason has done his worst: nor steel nor poison,
26   Malice domestic, foreign levy, nothing,
Can touch him further.

LADY MACBETH   Come on.
Gentle my lord, sleek o'er your rugged looks;
Be bright and jovial among your guests tonight.

MACBETH

30   So shall I, love; and so, I pray, be you.
31   Let your remembrance apply to Banquo;
32   Present him eminence both with eye and tongue:
33   Unsafe the while, that we must lave
Our honors in these flattering streams
35   And make our faces vizards to our hearts,
36   Disguising what they are.

LADY MACBETH   You must leave this.

---

12 *all* any   14 *scorched* slashed   15 *close* heal; *poor malice* inadequate evil
17 *frame . . . disjoint* structure of the universe collapse; *both the worlds*
heaven and earth   22 *torture* rack   23 *ecstasy* frenzy   26 *Malice domestic* native evil (rebellion)   31 *remembrance* reminder   32 *Present him eminence* do
him honor   33 *Unsafe . . . that* while we are unsafe; *lave* wash   35 *vizards*
masks   36 *leave* leave off, stop

MACBETH

    O, full of scorpions is my mind, dear wife.

    Thou know'st that Banquo, and his Fleance, lives.

LADY MACBETH

    But in them Nature's copy's not eterne.   39

MACBETH

    There's comfort yet; they are assailable.   40

    Then be thou jocund. Ere the bat hath flown

    His cloistered flight, ere to black Hecate's summons

    The shard-born beetle with his drowsy hums   43

    Hath rung night's yawning peal, there shall be done

    A deed of dreadful note.

LADY MACBETH   What's to be done?

MACBETH

    Be innocent of the knowledge, dearest chuck,   46

    Till thou applaud the deed. Come, seeling night,   47

    Scarf up the tender eye of pitiful day,   48

    And with thy bloody and invisible hand

    Cancel and tear to pieces that great bond   50

    Which keeps me pale. Light thickens, and the crow

    Makes wing to th' rooky wood.   52

    Good things of day begin to droop and drowse,

    Whiles night's black agents to their preys do rouse.

    Thou marvel'st at my words, but hold thee still;

    Things bad begun make strong themselves by ill.

    So prithee go with me.   *Exeunt.*

                       *

---

39 *Nature's copy* Nature's copyhold (their lease on life); *eterne* eternal 43 *shard-born* born in dung 46 *chuck* chick (term of affection) 47 *seeling* sewing up, hooding (from falconry) 48 *Scarf up* blindfold; *pitiful* pitying, compassionate 50 *bond* contract (Banquo's tenure of life) 52 *rooky* i.e., full of birds

∾ **III.3** *Enter three Murderers.*

FIRST MURDERER
    But who did bid thee join with us?
THIRD MURDERER   Macbeth.
SECOND MURDERER
2   He needs not our mistrust, since he delivers
3   Our offices and what we have to do
4   To the direction just.
FIRST MURDERER   Then stand with us.
    The west yet glimmers with some streaks of day.
6   Now spurs the lated traveler apace
7   To gain the timely inn, and near approaches
    The subject of our watch.
THIRD MURDERER   Hark, I hear horses.
BANQUO *Within*
    Give us a light there, ho!
SECOND MURDERER
10   Then 'tis he: the rest
11   That are within the note of expectation
    Already are i' th' court.
13 FIRST MURDERER   His horses go about.
THIRD MURDERER
    Almost a mile; but he does usually,
    So all men do, from hence to th' palace gate
    Make it their walk.
       Enter Banquo and Fleance, with a torch.
SECOND MURDERER   A light, a light!
THIRD MURDERER   'Tis he.
FIRST MURDERER   Stand to't.
BANQUO
20   It will be rain tonight.

III.3 Outside the castle   **2** *He . . . mistrust* we need not mistrust this man
3 *offices* duties   **4** *To . . . just* according to the precise instructions   **6** *lated*
belated   **7** *gain . . . inn* reach the inn in good time   **11** *within . . . expecta-*
tion on the list of those invited   **13** *His . . . about* i.e., he's walking his horses

FIRST MURDERER   Let it come down!
BANQUO
    O, treachery! Fly, good Fleance, fly, fly, fly!
                                        [Exit Fleance.]

    Thou mayst revenge – O slave!
        [Banquo slain.]
THIRD MURDERER
    Who did strike out the light?   23
FIRST MURDERER   Was't not the way?
THIRD MURDERER
    There's but one down: the son is fled.
SECOND MURDERER
    We have lost best half of our affair.
FIRST MURDERER
    Well, let's away, and say how much is done.   *Exeunt.*

                            ✳

❧ **III.4** *Banquet prepared. Enter Macbeth, Lady [Mac-*
        beth], Ross, Lennox, Lords, and Attendants.

MACBETH
    You know your own degrees – sit down: 1
    At first and last the hearty welcome.
LORDS
    Thanks to your majesty.
MACBETH
    Ourself will mingle with society   4
    And play the humble host.
    Our hostess keeps her state, but in best time   6
    We will require her welcome.
LADY MACBETH
    Pronounce it for me, sir, to all our friends,

---

23 *Was't . . . way* wasn't that the plan
    III.4 The great hall of the palace   **1** *degrees* relative rank, order of prece-
dence   **4** *society* the company   **6** *keeps her state* remains seated in her chair of
state

    For my heart speaks they are welcome.
      Enter First Murderer.

MACBETH

10   See, they encounter thee with their hearts' thanks.
    Both sides are even. Here I'll sit i' th' midst.
    Be large in mirth; anon we'll drink a measure
    The table round.
      [Goes to Murderer.]
    There's blood upon thy face.

FIRST MURDERER   'Tis Banquo's then.

MACBETH

    'Tis better thee without than he within.
    Is he dispatched?

FIRST MURDERER   My lord, his throat is cut:
    That I did for him.

MACBETH   Thou art the best o' th' cutthroats.
    Yet he's good that did the like for Fleance:

19   If thou didst it, thou art the nonpareil.

FIRST MURDERER

20   Most royal sir, Fleance is scaped.

MACBETH

21   Then comes my fit again. I had else been perfect;
22   Whole as the marble, founded as the rock,
23   As broad and general as the casing air.
24   But now I am cabined, cribbed, confined, bound in
25   To saucy doubts and fears. But Banquo's safe?

FIRST MURDERER

    Ay, my good lord. Safe in a ditch he bides,
27   With twenty trenchèd gashes on his head,
    The least a death to nature.

MACBETH   Thanks for that.

---

10 *encounter* greet   19 *nonpareil* absolute best   21 *perfect* flawless   22
founded solidly based   23 *broad and general* unconfined and omnipresent;
casing enveloping   24 *cabined* pent up; *cribbed* boxed in   25 *saucy* insolent;
safe safely disposed of (i.e., dead)   27 *trenchèd* deep-furrowed

There the grown serpent lies; the worm that's fled   29
Hath nature that in time will venom breed,   30
No teeth for th' present. Get thee gone. Tomorrow
We'll hear ourselves again.   *Exit Murderer.*   32
LADY MACBETH   My royal lord,
You do not give the cheer. The feast is sold   33
That is not often vouched, while 'tis a-making,   34
'Tis given with welcome. To feed were best at home;   35
From thence, the sauce to meat is ceremony: 36
Meeting were bare without it.
MACBETH   Sweet remembrancer!
Now good digestion wait on appetite,
And health on both.
LENNOX   May't please your highness sit.
MACBETH
Here had we now our country's honor roofed   40
Were the graced person of our Banquo present –
    Enter the Ghost of Banquo, and sits in Macbeth's place.
Who may I rather challenge for unkindness   42
Than pity for mischance.
ROSS   His absence, sir,
Lays blame upon his promise. Please't your highness
To grace us with your royal company?
MACBETH
The table's full.
LENNOX   Here is a place reserved, sir.
MACBETH
Where?
LENNOX
Here, my good lord. What is't that moves your high-
    ness?

---

29 *worm* snake   32 *hear ourselves* speak together   33 *give the cheer* toast the
company; *sold* i.e., not freely given   34 *vouched* affirmed   35 *To . . . home*
i.e., mere eating is best done at home   36 *From thence* away from home   42
challenge for accuse of

MACBETH
Which of you have done this?
LORDS
50 What, my good lord?
MACBETH
Thou canst not say I did it. Never shake
Thy gory locks at me.
ROSS
Gentlemen, rise. His highness is not well.
LADY MACBETH
Sit, worthy friends. My lord is often thus,
And hath been from his youth. Pray you keep seat.
The fit is momentary; upon a thought
He will again be well. If much you note him,
58 You shall offend him and extend his passion.
Feed, and regard him not. – Are you a man?
MACBETH
60 Ay, and a bold one, that dare look on that
Which might appall the devil.
LADY MACBETH   O proper stuff!
This is the very painting of your fear.
63 This is the air-drawn dagger which you said
64 Led you to Duncan. O, these flaws and starts,
65 Impostors to true fear, would well become
A woman's story at a winter's fire,
67 Authorized by her grandam. Shame itself!
Why do you make such faces? When all's done,
You look but on a stool.
MACBETH   Prithee see there!
70 Behold! Look! Lo! – How say you?
Why, what care I? If thou canst nod, speak too.
If charnel houses and our graves must send

---

58 *extend his passion* prolong his seizure   63 *air-drawn* i.e., fashioned of air
64 *flaws* outbursts   65 *to* in comparison with   67 *Authorized* told on the
authority of

Those that we bury back, our monuments   73
Shall be the maws of kites.   *[Exit Ghost.]*   74
LADY MACBETH   What, quite unmanned in folly?
MACBETH
If I stand here, I saw him.
LADY MACBETH   Fie, for shame!
MACBETH
Blood hath been shed ere now, i' th' olden time,
Ere humane statute purged the gentle weal;   77
Ay, and since too, murders have been performed
Too terrible for the ear. The time has been
That, when the brains were out, the man would die,   80
And there an end. But now they rise again,
With twenty mortal murders on their crowns,   82
And push us from our stools. This is more strange
Than such a murder is.
LADY MACBETH   My worthy lord,
Your noble friends do lack you.
MACBETH   I do forget.
Do not muse at me, my most worthy friends:
I have a strange infirmity, which is nothing
To those that know me. Come, love and health to all,
Then I'll sit down. Give me some wine, fill full.
I drink to th' general joy o' th' whole table,   90
And to our dear friend Banquo, whom we miss.
Would he were here!   *Enter Ghost.*   92
                        To all, and him we thirst,
And all to all.   93
LORDS   Our duties, and the pledge.
MACBETH
Avaunt, and quit my sight! Let the earth hide thee!
Thy bones are marrowless, thy blood is cold;

---

73 *our monuments* i.e., our only tombs **74** *maws of kites* bellies of ravens
77 *purged . . . weal* rendered the state civilized **82** *murders on their crowns*
murderous wounds on their heads **92** *him we thirst* him whom we long for
93 *all to all* each toast the others

96   Thou hast no speculation in those eyes
      Which thou dost glare with.
      LADY MACBETH   Think of this, good peers,
98   But as a thing of custom. 'Tis no other.
      Only it spoils the pleasure of the time.
      MACBETH
100   What man dare, I dare.
      Approach thou like the rugged Russian bear,
102   The armed rhinoceros, or th' Hyrcan tiger;
103   Take any shape but that, and my firm nerves
      Shall never tremble. Or be alive again
105   And dare me to the desert with thy sword.
106   If trembling I inhabit then, protest me
107   The baby of a girl. Hence, horrible shadow!
      Unreal mock'ry, hence!   *[Exit Ghost.]*
                            Why, so; being gone,
      I am a man again. – Pray you sit still.
      LADY MACBETH
110   You have displaced the mirth, broke the good meeting
111   With most admired disorder.
      MACBETH   Can such things be,
112   And overcome us like a summer's cloud
113   Without our special wonder? You make me strange
114   Even to the disposition that I owe,
      When now I think you can behold such sights
      And keep the natural ruby of your cheeks
      When mine is blanched with fear.
      ROSS   What sights, my lord?

------

96 *speculation* vision   98 *thing of custom* i.e., nothing out of the ordinary
102 *Hyrcan* from Hyrcania (classical name for the area on the south coast of
the Caspian Sea; its tigers were proverbially fierce)   103 *but that* i.e., but
that of Banquo's ghost   105 *dare . . . desert* challenge me to fight you in the
desert   106 *If . . . inhabit* if I make a habit of trembling   107 *The . . . girl* a
baby girl, or a girl's doll   111 *admired* amazing   112 *overcome* pass over
113–14 *You . . . owe* you estrange me from my true nature (as a brave man)
114 *owe* own

LADY MACBETH

    I pray you speak not: he grows worse and worse;
    Question enrages him. At once, good night.
    Stand not upon the order of your going,   120
    But go at once.

LENNOX   Good night and better health
    Attend his majesty.

LADY MACBETH   A kind good night to all.

                                    Exeunt Lords.

MACBETH

    It will have blood, they say: blood will have blood.
    Stones have been known to move and trees to speak;
    Augurs and understood relations have   125
    By maggotpies and choughs and rooks brought forth   126
    The secret'st man of blood. What is the night?   127

LADY MACBETH

    Almost at odds with morning, which is which.

MACBETH

    How say'st thou, that Macduff denies his person
    At our great bidding?   *130*

LADY MACBETH   Did you send to him, sir?

MACBETH

    I hear it by the way; but I will send.   131
    There's not a one of them but in his house
    I keep a servant fee'd. I will tomorrow,   133
    And betimes I will, to the weïrd sisters.   134
    More shall they speak, for now I am bent to know   135
    By the worst means the worst. For mine own good
    All causes shall give way. I am in blood
    Stepped in so far that, should I wade no more,

---

120 *Stand . . . going* i.e., don't bother about precedence 125 *Augurs* au-
guries; *understood relations* comprehensible relations of causes to effects
126 *maggotpies, choughs* magpies, crows (both, like *rooks,* capable of imitating
speech, and all three birds of ill omen) 127 *secret'st man of blood* best-hid-
den murderer 131 *by the way* casually; *send* send a messenger 133 *fee'd*
paid to spy 134 *betimes* (1) speedily, (2) early 135 *bent* determined

Returning were as tedious as go o'er.
140   Strange things I have in head, that will to hand,
141   Which must be acted ere they may be scanned.
LADY MACBETH
142   You lack the season of all natures, sleep.
MACBETH
143   Come, we'll to sleep. My strange and self-abuse
144   Is the initiate fear that wants hard use.
We are yet but young in deed.   *Exeunt.*

＊

～ **III.5** *Thunder. Enter the three Witches, meeting
Hecate.*

FIRST WITCH
Why, how now, Hecate? You look angerly.
HECATE
2   Have I not reason, beldams as you are,
Saucy and overbold? How did you dare
To trade and traffic with Macbeth
In riddles and affairs of death;
And I, the mistress of your charms,
7   The close contriver of all harms,
8   Was never called to bear my part
Or show the glory of our art?
10   And, which is worse, all you have done
11   Hath been but for a wayward son,
Spiteful and wrathful, who, as others do,
Loves for his own ends, not for you.
But make amends now: get you gone
15   And at the pit of Acheron

---

141 *scanned* analyzed   142 *season* (1) the best time (when nature is "in season"), (2) the seasoning (what makes life palatable)   143 *self-abuse* delusion,
hallucination   144 *initiate* beginner's; *wants hard use* needs much practice
   III.5 An open place (a non-Shakespearean scene)   2 *beldams* hags,
witches   7 *close* secret   8 *bear my part* participate   11 *wayward* willful, dis-
obedient   15 *Acheron* one of the rivers of Hades

Meet me i' th' morning. Thither he
Will come to know his destiny.
Your vessels and your spells provide,   18
Your charms and everything beside.
I am for th' air. This night I'll spend   20
Unto a dismal and a fatal end.
Great business must be wrought ere noon.
Upon the corner of the moon
There hangs a vap'rous drop profound;   24
I'll catch it ere it come to ground;
And that, distilled by magic sleights,   26
Shall raise such artificial sprites   27
As by the strength of their illusion
Shall draw him on to his confusion.   29
He shall spurn fate, scorn death, and bear   30
His hopes 'bove wisdom, grace, and fear;
And you all know security   32
Is mortals' chiefest enemy.
      Music, and a song.
[FIRST SPIRIT *Within*]
    Hecate, Hecate, Hecate, O come away!
HECATE
    Hark, I am called. My little spirit, see,
    Sits in a foggy cloud and stays for me.
FIRST SPIRIT *Within*
    Come away, Hecate, Hecate, O come away!
HECATE
    I come, I come, with all the speed I may.
    Where's Stadling?
SECOND SPIRIT *Within*
                        Here.
HECATE   Where's Puckle?
SECOND SPIRIT *Within*   Here.

---

18 *vessels* cauldrons **24** *a vap'rous drop profound* a misty "exhalation" with deep, hidden properties **26** *sleights* artifices **27** *artificial* (1) deceitful, (2) produced by artifice **29** *confusion* damnation **32** *security* overconfidence

FIRST SPIRIT *Within*
40 And Hopper too, and Hellway too;
41 We want but you, we want but you!
Come away, make up the count.

HECATE
43 I will but 'noint, and then I mount;
I will but 'noint, and then I mount.

FIRST SPIRIT *Within*
Here comes down one to fetch his due,
46 A kiss, a cull, a sip of blood;
And why thou stay'st so long I muse,
Since the air's so sweet and good.

HECATE
O, art thou come? What news?

SECOND SPIRIT *Within*
50 All goes for our delight.
Either come, or else refuse.
Now I am furnished for the flight;
Now I go, and now I fly,
Malkin my sweet spirit and I.

THIRD SPIRIT *Within*
O what a dainty pleasure's this,
To sail i' th' air while the moon shines fair,
To sing, to toy, to dance, and kiss.
Over woods, high rocks and mountains,
Over hills and misty fountains,
60 Over steeples, towers and turrets
We fly by night 'mongst troops of spirits.
No ring of bells to our ears sounds,
No howls of wolves nor yelps of hounds,
64 No, nor the noise of water's breach,
Nor cannons' throats our height can reach.

FIRST SPIRIT *Within* [Exit Hecate.]
Come, let's make haste, she'll soon be back again.

---

41 *We . . . you* only you are missing 43 *'noint* anoint myself (with a magic ointment) 46 *cull* hug 64 *water's breach* breaking waves

SECOND SPIRIT   *Within*
> But whilst she moves through the foggy air,
> Let's to the cave and our dire charms prepare.

> > > > > > > > > > > > > > > > > *Exeunt.*

*

❧ **III.6** *Enter Lennox and another Lord.*

LENNOX
> My former speeches have but hit your thoughts,   1
> Which can interpret farther. Only I say   2
> Things have been strangely borne. The gracious Duncan
> Was pitied of Macbeth. Marry, he was dead.
> And the right valiant Banquo walked too late;
> Whom, you may say, if't please you, Fleance killed,
> For Fleance fled. Men must not walk too late.
> Who cannot want the thought how monstrous   8
> It was for Malcolm and for Donalbain
> To kill their gracious father? Damnèd fact,   10
> How it did grieve Macbeth! Did he not straight,
> In pious rage, the two delinquents tear
> That were the slaves of drink and thralls of sleep?   13
> Was not that nobly done? Ay, and wisely too,
> For 'twould have angered any heart alive
> To hear the men deny't. So that I say
> He has borne all things well; and I do think   17
> That, had he Duncan's sons under his key –
> As, an't please heaven, he shall not – they should find   19
> What 'twere to kill a father. So should Fleance.   20
> But peace; for from broad words, and 'cause he failed   21
> His presence at the tyrant's feast, I hear
> Macduff lives in disgrace. Sir, can you tell
> Where he bestows himself?

III.6 Somewhere in Scotland **1** *My former speeches* what I have just said; *hit* coincided with **2** *interpret farther* draw their own conclusions **8** *cannot . . . thought* can avoid thinking **10** *fact* crime **13** *thralls* slaves **17** *borne* carried off **19** *an't* if it **21** *from broad words* because of his blunt speech

LORD   The son of Duncan,
25   From whom this tyrant holds the due of birth,
     Lives in the English court, and is received
     Of the most pious Edward with such grace
     That the malevolence of fortune nothing
29   Takes from his high respect. Thither Macduff
30   Is gone to pray the holy king upon his aid
31   To wake Northumberland and warlike Siward;
     That by the help of these (with Him above
     To ratify the work) we may again
     Give to our tables meat, sleep to our nights,
     Free from our feasts and banquets bloody knives,
36   Do faithful homage and receive free honors –
     All which we pine for now. And this report
     Hath so exasperate the king that he
     Prepares for some attempt of war.
40   LENNOX   Sent he to Macduff?
     LORD
     He did; and with an absolute "Sir, not I,"
42   The cloudy messenger turns me his back
     And hums, as who should say, "You'll rue the time
44   That clogs me with this answer."
     LENNOX   And that well might
45   Advise him to a caution t' hold what distance
     His wisdom can provide. Some holy angel
     Fly to the court of England and unfold
     His message ere he come, that a swift blessing
     May soon return to this our suffering country
50   Under a hand accursed.
     LORD   I'll send my prayers with him.

                                        Exeunt.

                          ✽

---

25 *holds . . . birth* withholds his birthright   29 *his high respect* the great esteem
for him   30 *upon his aid* on Malcolm's behalf   31 *Northumberland, Siward*
(the English county bordering Scotland, and the family name of the Earl of
Northumberland)   36 *free* untainted   42 *cloudy* angry   44 *clogs* burdens   45–
46 *Advise . . . provide* caution him to keep as safe a distance as he can manage

∾ **IV.1** *Thunder. Enter the three Witches.*

FIRST WITCH
      Thrice the brindled cat hath mewed.   1
SECOND WITCH
      Thrice, and once the hedgepig whined.
THIRD WITCH
      Harpier cries – 'Tis time, 'tis time!   3
FIRST WITCH
      Round about the cauldron go;
      In the poisoned entrails throw.
      Toad, that under cold stone
      Days and nights has thirty-one
      Sweltered venom sleeping got,   8
      Boil thou first i' th' charmèd pot.
ALL
      Double, double toil and trouble,   10
      Fire burn and cauldron bubble.
SECOND WITCH
      Fillet of a fenny snake,   12
      In the cauldron boil and bake;
      Eye of newt, and toe of frog,
      Wool of bat, and tongue of dog,
      Adder's fork, and blindworm's sting,   16
      Lizard's leg, and owlet's wing –
      For a charm of powerful trouble
      Like a hellbroth boil and bubble.
ALL
      Double, double toil and trouble,   20
      Fire burn and cauldron bubble.
THIRD WITCH
      Scale of dragon, tooth of wolf,

IV.1 The witches' cave **1** *brindled* striped **3** *Harpier* (a familiar spirit, like Graymalkin and Paddock) **8** *Sweltered . . . got* poisonous sweat generated while asleep **12** *fenny* marsh **16** *fork* forked tongue; *blindworm* adder

23	Witch's mummy, maw and gulf
24	Of the ravined salt-sea shark,
	Root of hemlock digged i' th' dark,
	Liver of blaspheming Jew,
	Gall of goat, and slips of yew
	Slivered in the moon's eclipse,
	Nose of Turk, and Tartar's lips,
30	Finger of birth-strangled babe
31	Ditch-delivered by a drab
32	Make the gruel thick and slab.
33	Add thereto a tiger's chawdron
	For th' ingredience of our cauldron.

ALL

    Double, double toil and trouble,
    Fire burn and cauldron bubble.

SECOND WITCH

    Cool it with a baboon's blood,
38   Then the charm is firm and good.

Enter Hecate and the other three Witches.

HECATE

    O, well done! I commend your pains,
40   And every one shall share i' th' gains.
    And now about the cauldron sing
    Like elves and fairies in a ring,
    Enchanting all that you put in.

Music and a song.

HECATE

    Black spirits and white,
    Red spirits and gray
46   Mingle, mingle, mingle,
    You that mingle may.

---

23 *mummy* mummified flesh; *maw and gulf* devouring stomach; *gulf* anything voracious 24 *ravined* ravenous 31 *Ditch-delivered* born in a ditch; *drab* whore 32 *slab* thick, semiliquid 33 *chawdron* guts 38 **s.d. to 64** (the Hecate section is a non-Shakespearean addition) 46 *Mingle* mix together (but with an obscene overtone: have intercourse; see l. 49)

FOURTH WITCH
>Tiffin, Tiffin,
>Keep it stiff in.

FIFTH WITCH
>Firedrake Pucky,   50
>Make it lucky.

HECATE
>Liar Robin,
>You must bob in.

CHORUS
>Around, around, around, about, about,
>All ill come running in, all good keep out.

FOURTH WITCH
>Here's the blood of a bat.

HECATE
>O put in that, put in that.

FIFTH WITCH
>Here's lizard's brain.

HECATE
>Put in a grain.

FOURTH WITCH
>Here's juice of toad, here's oil of adder,   60
>That will make the charm grow madder.

FIFTH WITCH
>Put in all these, 'twill raise the stench.

HECATE
>Nay, here's three ounces of a red-haired wench.

CHORUS
>Around, around, around, about, about,
>All ill come running in, all good keep out.
>
>>[Exeunt Hecate and the three Singers.]

SECOND WITCH
>By the pricking of my thumbs,
>Something wicked this way comes.

---

50 *Firedrake* will-o'-the-wisp

Open locks,
Whoever knocks!
Enter Macbeth.

MACBETH

70   How now, you secret, black, and midnight hags,
      What is't you do?

ALL   A deed without a name.

MACBETH

72 · I conjure you by that which you profess,
      Howe'er you come to know it, answer me.
      Though you untie the winds and let them fight
75   Against the churches, though the yeasty waves
      Confound and swallow navigation up,
77   Though bladed corn be lodged and trees blown down,
      Though castles topple on their warders' heads,
79   Though palaces and pyramids do slope
80   Their heads to their foundations, though the treasure
81   Of Nature's germens tumble all together
82   Even till destruction sicken, answer me
      To what I ask you.

FIRST WITCH   Speak.
SECOND WITCH   Demand.
THIRD WITCH   We'll answer.
FIRST WITCH
      Say if thou'dst rather hear it from our mouths
85   Or from our masters.
MACBETH   Call 'em. Let me see 'em.
FIRST WITCH
                  Pour in sow's blood, that hath eaten
87   Her nine farrow; grease that's sweaten ·

---

70 *black* evil, malevolent **72** *that . . . profess* your profession, witchcraft
75 *yeasty* foaming **77** *bladed . . . lodged* ripe wheat be flattened **79** *slope*
bend **81** *Nature's germens* the essential seeds of nature **82** *sicken* surfeit
85 *masters* instruments, agents, experts (the spirits through whom they com-
municate with the occult world – a master is a skilled workman) **87** *nine
farrow* litter of nine; *sweaten* exuded

From the murderer's gibbet throw
Into the flame.

ALL   Come, high or low,
Thyself and office deftly show.   90

Thunder. First Apparition, an Armed Head.

MACBETH
Tell me, thou unknown power –

FIRST WITCH   He knows thy thought:
Hear his speech, but say thou naught.

FIRST APPARITION
Macbeth, Macbeth, Macbeth, beware Macduff,
Beware the Thane of Fife. Dismiss me. Enough.

He descends.

MACBETH
Whate'er thou art, for thy good caution thanks:
Thou hast harped my fear aright. But one word more –   96

FIRST WITCH
He will not be commanded. Here's another,
More potent than the first.

Thunder. Second Apparition, a Bloody Child.

SECOND APPARITION
Macbeth, Macbeth, Macbeth –

MACBETH
Had I three ears, I'd hear thee.   *100*

SECOND APPARITION
Be bloody, bold, and resolute. Laugh to scorn
The pow'r of man, for none of woman born
Shall harm Macbeth.   *Descends.*

MACBETH
Then live, Macduff, what need I fear of thee?
But yet I'll make assurance double sure
And take a bond of fate. Thou shalt not live,   106
That I may tell pale-hearted fear it lies

---

90 *office* function   **96** *harped* hit the tune of   **106** *take a bond of* secure a
guarantee from

And sleep in spite of thunder.
> *Thunder. Third Apparition, a Child Crowned, with a*
> *tree in his hand.*

                           What is this
That rises like the issue of a king

110 And wears upon his baby brow the round
And top of sovereignty?
ALL   Listen, but speak not to't.
THIRD APPARITION
Be lion-mettled, proud, and take no care
Who chafes, who frets, or where conspirers are.
Macbeth shall never vanquished be until
Great Birnam Wood to high Dunsinane Hill
Shall come against him.   *Descends.*
MACBETH   That will never be.

117 Who can impress the forest, bid the tree
118 Unfix his earthbound root? Sweet bodements, good.
Rebellious dead rise never till the Wood
120 Of Birnam rise, and our high-placed Macbeth
121 Shall live the lease of nature, pay his breath
To time and mortal custom. Yet my heart
Throbs to know one thing. Tell me, if your art
124 Can tell so much: Shall Banquo's issue ever
Reign in this kingdom?
ALL   Seek to know no more.
MACBETH
I will be satisfied. Deny me this,
And an eternal curse fall on you! Let me know.
Why sinks that cauldron? and what noise is this?
> *Hautboys.*

FIRST WITCH   Show!
130 SECOND WITCH   Show!
THIRD WITCH   Show!

110–11 *round . . . top* crown 117 *impress* conscript 118 *bodements*
prophecies 121 *lease of nature* full life span 121–22 *pay . . . custom* be obligated only to age and normal death 124 *issue* offspring

ALL

        Show his eyes, and grieve his heart,
        Come like shadows, so depart.   133
    A show of eight Kings and Banquo, last [King] with a
    glass in his hand.

MACBETH

  Thou art too like the spirit of Banquo. Down!
  Thy crown does sear mine eyeballs. And thy hair,
  Thou other gold-bound brow, is like the first.
  A third is like the former. Filthy hags,
  Why do you show me this? A fourth? Start, eyes!   138
  What, will the line stretch out to th' crack of doom?
  Another yet? A seventh? I'll see no more.   *140*
  And yet the eighth appears, who bears a glass
  Which shows me many more; and some I see
  That twofold balls and treble scepters carry.   143
  Horrible sight! Now I see 'tis true;
  For the blood-boltered Banquo smiles upon me   145
  And points at them for his. What? Is this so?
                      [Exeunt apparitions.]

FIRST WITCH

        Ay, sir, all this is so. But why   147
        Stands Macbeth thus amazedly?
        Come, sisters, cheer we up his sprites   149
        And show the best of our delights.   *150*
        I'll charm the air to give a sound
        While you perform your antic round,   152
        That this great king may kindly say
        Our duties did his welcome pay.
             Music. The Witches dance, and vanish.

MACBETH

  Where are they? Gone? Let this pernicious hour

---

133 s.d. *glass* mirror   138 *Start* burst, start from your sockets   143
twofold . . . scepters two orbs and three scepters (the British royal insignia)
145 *blood-boltered* matted with blood   147–54 (a non-Shakespearean addition)   149 *sprites* spirits   152 *antic round* grotesque dance

Stand aye accursèd in the calendar.
Come in, without there!
   Enter Lennox.

LENNOX   What's your grace's will?

MACBETH
Saw you the weïrd sisters?

LENNOX   No, my lord.

MACBETH
Came they not by you?

LENNOX   No indeed, my lord.

MACBETH

160   Infected be the air whereon they ride,
And damned all those that trust them! I did hear
The galloping of horse. Who was't came by?

LENNOX
'Tis two or three, my lord, that bring you word
Macduff is fled to England.

MACBETH   Fled to England?

LENNOX
Ay, my good lord.

MACBETH   *[Aside]*

166   Time, thou anticipat'st my dread exploits.
167   The flighty purpose never is o'ertook
Unless the deed go with it. From this moment
169   The very firstlings of my heart shall be
170   The firstlings of my hand. And even now,
To crown my thoughts with acts, be it thought and
   done:
The castle of Macduff I will surprise,
Seize upon Fife, give to th' edge o' th' sword
His wife, his babes, and all unfortunate souls
175   That trace him in his line. No boasting like a fool;

---

166 *anticipat'st* forestall   **167** *flighty* fleeting   **169–70** *firstlings . . . my hand*
i.e., I shall act at the moment I feel the first impulse   **175** *trace* follow; *line*
family line

This deed I'll do before this purpose cool.
But no more sights. *[To Lennox]* Where are these gen-
  tlemen?
Come, bring me where they are.   *Exeunt.*

*

∾ **IV.2** *Enter Macduff's Wife, her Son, and Ross.*

LADY MACDUFF
  What had he done to make him fly the land?
ROSS
  You must have patience, madam.
LADY MACDUFF   He had none.
  His flight was madness. When our actions do not,
  Our fears do make us traitors.   4
ROSS   You know not
  Whether it was his wisdom or his fear.
LADY MACDUFF
  Wisdom? To leave his wife, to leave his babes,
  His mansion and his titles in a place   7
  From whence himself does fly? He loves us not,
  He wants the natural touch. For the poor wren,   9
  The most diminutive of birds, will fight,   10
  Her young ones in her nest, against the owl.
  All is the fear and nothing is the love,
  As little is the wisdom, where the flight
  So runs against all reason.   14
ROSS   My dearest coz,
  I pray you school yourself. But for your husband,   15
  He is noble, wise, judicious, and best knows   16
  The fits o' th' season. I dare not speak much further,

IV.2 Macduff's castle at Fife **4** *traitors* i.e., betray our interests **7** *titles*
rights, what he is entitled to **9** *wants* lacks **14** *coz* (from "cousin," an af-
fectionate diminutive) **15** *school* control **16–17** *knows . . . season* understands the violent conditions of the time

18 But cruel are the times when we are traitors
19 And do not know ourselves; when we hold rumor
20 From what we fear, yet know not what we fear,
   But float upon a wild and violent sea
22 Each way and none. I take my leave of you,
   Shall not be long but I'll be here again.
24 Things at the worst will cease, or else climb upward
   To what they were before. *[To the Son]* My pretty cousin,
   Blessing upon you.

LADY MACDUFF
   Fathered he is, and yet he's fatherless.

ROSS
   I am so much a fool, should I stay longer
29 It would be my disgrace and your discomfort.
30 I take my leave at once.   *Exit.*

LADY MACDUFF
   Sirrah, your father's dead;
   And what will you do now? How will you live?

SON
   As birds do, mother.

LADY MACDUFF   What, with worms and flies?

SON
   With what I get, I mean; and so do they.

LADY MACDUFF
35 Poor bird, thou'dst never fear the net nor lime,
36 The pitfall nor the gin.

SON
   Why should I, mother? Poor birds they are not set for.
   My father is not dead for all your saying.

LADY MACDUFF
   Yes, he is dead. How wilt thou do for a father?

18–19 *we . . . ourselves* we are considered traitors and do not know that we are 19–20 *hold . . . fear* believe rumors based on what we fear 22 *Each way and none* i.e., move every which way but in no settled direction 24 *will cease* i.e., can get no worse 29 *my disgrace* (because he would weep) 35 *lime* birdlime (a sticky substance used to catch birds) 36 *gin* trap

SON   Nay, how will you do for a husband?   40
LADY MACDUFF   Why, I can buy me twenty at any market.
SON   Then you'll buy 'em to sell again.   42
LADY MACDUFF
  Thou speak'st with all thy wit; and yet, i' faith,   43
  With wit enough for thee.
SON   Was my father a traitor, mother?
LADY MACDUFF   Ay, that he was.
SON   What is a traitor?
LADY MACDUFF   Why, one that swears and lies.   48
SON   And be all traitors that do so?
LADY MACDUFF   Every one that does so is a traitor and   50
  must be hanged.
SON   And must they all be hanged that swear and lie?
LADY MACDUFF   Every one.
SON   Who must hang them?
LADY MACDUFF   Why, the honest men.
SON   Then the liars and swearers are fools, for there are
  liars and swearers enow to beat the honest men and   57
  hang up them.
LADY MACDUFF   Now God help thee, poor monkey! But
  how wilt thou do for a father?   60
SON   If he were dead, you'd weep for him. If you would
  not, it were a good sign that I should quickly have a
  new father.
LADY MACDUFF   Poor prattler, how thou talk'st!
  Enter a Messenger.
MESSENGER
  Bless you, fair dame. I am not to you known,
  Though in your state of honor I am perfect.   66
  I doubt some danger does approach you nearly.   67
  If you will take a homely man's advice,   68

---

42 *sell* deceive them   43–44 *with . . . thee* indeed, you are witty enough
48 *swears and lies* takes a vow and violates it   57 *enow* enough   66 *in . . .
perfect* I am well aware of your nobility and virtue; *state of honor* (1) high
status, (2) honorable character   67 *doubt* fear   68 *homely* plain

Be not found here. Hence with your little ones.
70 To fright you thus methinks I am too savage;
71 To do worse to you were fell cruelty,
72 Which is too nigh your person. Heaven preserve you!
    I dare abide no longer.   *Exit.*
LADY MACDUFF   Whither should I fly?
    I have done no harm. But I remember now
    I am in this earthly world, where to do harm
    Is often laudable, to do good sometime
    Accounted dangerous folly. Why then, alas,
    Do I put up that womanly defense
    To say I have done no harm?
        Enter Murderers.   What are these faces?
MURDERER
80 Where is your husband?
LADY MACDUFF
    I hope in no place so unsanctified
    Where such as thou mayst find him.
MURDERER   He's a traitor.
SON
83 Thou liest, thou shag-haired villain!
MURDERER   What, you egg!
        [Stabs him.]
84 Young fry of treachery!
SON   He has killed me, mother.
    Run away, I pray you!
        [Dies.]   *Exit [Lady Macduff], crying "Murder"*
                                [pursued by Murderers].

                            *

---

71 *fell* deadly   72 *nigh* near (i.e., I frighten you to save you from the worse
cruelty threatening you)   83 *shag-haired* unkempt, uncouth   84, 84 *egg, fry*
offspring of birds and fish, respectively

∽ **IV.3** *Enter Malcolm and Macduff.*

MALCOLM
  Let us seek out some desolate shade, and there
  Weep our sad bosoms empty.
MACDUFF   Let us rather
  Hold fast the mortal sword and, like good men,   3
  Bestride our downfall birthdom. Each new morn   4
  New widows howl, new orphans cry, new sorrows
  Strike heaven on the face, that it resounds
  As if it felt with Scotland and yelled out
  Like syllable of dolor.   8
MALCOLM   What I believe, I'll wail;
  What know, believe; and what I can redress,
  As I shall find the time to friend, I will.   10
  What you have spoke, it may be so perchance.
  This tyrant, whose sole name blisters our tongues,   12
  Was once thought honest; you have loved him well;
  He hath not touched you yet. I am young, but some-
    thing
  You may deserve of him through me, and wisdom   15
  To offer up a weak, poor, innocent lamb
  T' appease an angry god.
MACDUFF
  I am not treacherous.
MALCOLM   But Macbeth is.
  A good and virtuous nature may recoil   19
  In an imperial charge. But I shall crave your pardon.   20
  That which you are, my thoughts cannot transpose: 21
  Angels are bright still though the brightest fell;   22

IV.3 In England, at the court of King Edward the Confessor **3** *fast* tightly;
mortal deadly **4** *downfall* fallen; *birthdom* (1) homeland, (2) inheritance
8 *Like . . . dolor* the same cry of grief **10** *to friend* befriending me (i.e., pro-
pitious) **12** *sole name* name alone **15** *wisdom* you may consider it wise
19 *recoil* hold back, withdraw **20** *In . . . charge* (1) in an imperial military
engagement, (2) under royal orders **21** *transpose* change **22** *the brightest*
Lucifer

23   Though all things foul would wear the brows of grace,
      Yet grace must still look so.

MACDUFF   I have lost my hopes.

MALCOLM
      Perchance even there where I did find my doubts.
26   Why in that rawness left you wife and child,
      Those precious motives, those strong knots of love,
      Without leave-taking? I pray you,
29   Let not my jealousies be your dishonors,
30   But mine own safeties. You may be rightly just
      Whatever I shall think.

MACDUFF   Bleed, bleed, poor country!
32   Great tyranny, lay thou thy basis sure,
      For goodness dare not check thee; wear thou thy
         wrongs,
34   The title is affeered! Fare thee well, lord.
      I would not be the villain that thou think'st
      For the whole space that's in the tyrant's grasp
      And the rich East to boot.

MALCOLM   Be not offended.
38   I speak not as in absolute fear of you.
      I think our country sinks beneath the yoke,
40   It weeps, it bleeds, and each new day a gash
41   Is added to her wounds. I think withal
      There would be hands uplifted in my right;
43   And here from gracious England have I offer
      Of goodly thousands. But, for all this,
      When I shall tread upon the tyrant's head
      Or wear it on my sword, yet my poor country
      Shall have more vices than it had before,
      More suffer, and more sundry ways than ever,
      By him that shall succeed.

---

23 *wear . . . grace* put on the appearance of goodness   26 *rawness* sudden-
ness, rudeness   29 *jealousies* suspicions   32 *basis* foundation   34 *The title is
affeered* (1) your claim is legally confirmed, (2) the valid claimant is fright-
ened (afeard) of you   38 *as . . . fear* entirely in fear   41 *withal* moreover
43 *England* the King of England

MACDUFF   What should he be?

MALCOLM

It is myself I mean, in whom I know   50
All the particulars of vice so grafted   51
That, when they shall be opened, black Macbeth   52
Will seem as pure as snow, and the poor state
Esteem him as a lamb, being compared
With my confineless harms.   55

MACDUFF   Not in the legions
Of horrid hell can come a devil more damned
In evils to top Macbeth.

MALCOLM   I grant him bloody,
Luxurious, avaricious, false, deceitful,   58
Sudden, malicious, smacking of every sin   59
That has a name. But there's no bottom, none,   60
In my voluptuousness. Your wives, your daughters,
Your matrons, and your maids could not fill up
The cistern of my lust; and my desire
All continent impediments would o'erbear   64
That did oppose my will. Better Macbeth
Than such an one to reign.

MACDUFF   Boundless intemperance
In nature is a tyranny. It hath been   67
Th' untimely emptying of the happy throne
And fall of many kings. But fear not yet
To take upon you what is yours. You may   70
Convey your pleasures in a spacious plenty   71
And yet seem cold – the time you may so hoodwink.
We have willing dames enough. There cannot be   73
That vulture in you to devour so many
As will to greatness dedicate themselves,
Finding it so inclined.

---

51 *particulars* varieties; *grafted* implanted   52 *opened* revealed   55 *confineless*
limitless   58 *Luxurious* lecherous   59 *Sudden* violent   64 *continent* re-
straining   67 *nature* human nature   71 *Convey* manage   73–76 *There . . .
inclined* i.e., when you are king, more women will willingly offer to serve
your lust than you can possibly consume

MALCOLM   With this there grows
77 In my most ill-composed affection such
78 A stanchless avarice that, were I king,
79 I should cut off the nobles for their lands,
80 Desire his jewels, and this other's house,
    And my more-having would be as a sauce
82 To make me hunger more, that I should forge
    Quarrels unjust against the good and loyal,
    Destroying them for wealth.
MACDUFF   This avarice
    Sticks deeper, grows with more pernicious root
86 Than summer-seeming lust, and it hath been
87 The sword of our slain kings. Yet do not fear.
88 Scotland hath foisons to fill up your will
89 Of your mere own. All these are portable,
90 With other graces weighed.
MALCOLM
    But I have none. The king-becoming graces,
    As justice, verity, temp'rance, stableness,
93 Bounty, perseverance, mercy, lowliness,
    Devotion, patience, courage, fortitude,
95 I have no relish of them, but abound
96 In the division of each several crime,
    Acting in many ways. Nay, had I pow'r, I should
    Pour the sweet milk of concord into hell,
99 Uproar the universal peace, confound
100 All unity on earth.
MACDUFF   O Scotland, Scotland!
MALCOLM
    If such a one be fit to govern, speak.
    I am as I have spoken.
MACDUFF   Fit to govern?

---

77 *ill-composed affection* ill-regulated passion 78 *stanchless* insatiable 79
cut off execute 82 *that I should forge* so that I would fabricate 86 *summer-
seeming* i.e., transitory and hot 87 *sword . . . slain* cause of death of our 88
foisons plenty 89 *mere* very; *portable* bearable 93 *lowliness* humility 95
relish trace 96 *division* variations 99 *Uproar* throw into chaos

No, not to live! O nation miserable,
With an untitled tyrant bloody-sceptered,   104
When shalt thou see thy wholesome days again,
Since that the truest issue of thy throne
By his own interdiction stands accursed   107
And does blaspheme his breed? Thy royal father   108
Was a most sainted king; the queen that bore thee,
Oft'ner upon her knees than on her feet,   *110*
Died every day she lived. Fare thee well.   111
These evils thou repeat'st upon thyself
Hath banished me from Scotland. O my breast,
Thy hope ends here.

MALCOLM   Macduff, this noble passion,
Child of integrity, hath from my soul
Wiped the black scruples, reconciled my thoughts   116
To thy good truth and honor. Devilish Macbeth
By many of these trains hath sought to win me   118
Into his power; and modest wisdom plucks me   119
From overcredulous haste; but God above   *120*
Deal between thee and me, for even now
I put myself to thy direction and
Unspeak mine own detraction, here abjure
The taints and blames I laid upon myself
For strangers to my nature. I am yet   125
Unknown to woman, never was forsworn,
Scarcely have coveted what was mine own,
At no time broke my faith, would not betray
The devil to his fellow, and delight
No less in truth than life. My first false speaking   *130*
Was this upon myself. What I am truly
Is thine and my poor country's to command;
Whither indeed, before thy here-approach,

---

104 *untitled* not entitled to rule **107** *interdiction* prohibition **108** *blaspheme his breed* slander his heritage **111** *Died* i.e., turned away from this life **116** *scruples* doubts **118** *trains* plots **119** *modest* cautious; *plucks* restrains **125** *For* as **125–26** *am . . . woman* have never slept with a woman

Old Siward with ten thousand warlike men
135   Already at a point was setting forth.
136   Now we'll together; and the chance of goodness
        Be like our warranted quarrel. Why are you silent?

MACDUFF
        Such welcome and unwelcome things at once
        'Tis hard to reconcile.
            Enter a Doctor.

MALCOLM
140   Well, more anon. – Comes the king forth, I pray you?

DOCTOR
        Ay, sir. There are a crew of wretched souls
142   That stay his cure. Their malady convinces
143   The great assay of art; but at his touch,
        Such sanctity hath heaven given his hand,
        They presently amend.

MALCOLM   I thank you, doctor.
                                    Exit [Doctor].

MACDUFF
146   What's the disease he means?

MALCOLM   'Tis called the evil.
        A most miraculous work in this good king,
        Which often since my here-remain in England
        I have seen him do: how he solicits heaven
150   Himself best knows, but strangely visited people,
        All swoll'n and ulcerous, pitiful to the eye,
152   The mere despair of surgery, he cures,
153   Hanging a golden stamp about their necks,
154   Put on with holy prayers, and 'tis spoken

---

135 *at a point* fully prepared   136 *we'll together* we'll go on together   136–
37 *the chance . . . quarrel* let our good fortune match our just cause   140
anon soon   142 *stay* await; *convinces* overwhelms   143 *assay of art* attempts
of (medical) science   146 *the evil* the King's Evil, scrofula (a painful inflam-
mation of the lymph nodes, often accompanied by ulcerations)   150
strangely visited seriously afflicted   152 *mere* utter   153 *stamp* coin or medal
154–56 *'tis . . . benediction* it is said that he bequeaths the healing power to
the monarchs who succeed him

To the succeeding royalty he leaves
The healing benediction. With this strange virtue,   156
He hath a heavenly gift of prophecy,
And sundry blessings hang about his throne
That speak him full of grace.   159
    Enter Ross.
MACDUFF   See who comes here.
MALCOLM
My countryman; but yet I know him not.   160
MACDUFF
My ever gentle cousin, welcome hither.
MALCOLM
I know him now. Good God betimes remove   162
The means that makes us strangers.
ROSS   Sir, amen.
MACDUFF
Stands Scotland where it did?
ROSS   Alas, poor country,
Almost afraid to know itself. It cannot
Be called our mother but our grave, where nothing   166
But who knows nothing is once seen to smile;
Where sighs and groans, and shrieks that rend the air,
Are made, not marked; where violent sorrow seems   169
A modern ecstasy. The dead man's knell   170
Is there scarce asked for who, and good men's lives   171
Expire before the flowers in their caps,
Dying or ere they sicken.   173
MACDUFF   O, relation
Too nice, and yet too true!   174
MALCOLM   What's the newest grief?
ROSS
That of an hour's age doth hiss the speaker;   175

---

156 *virtue* power **159** *speak* declare **162** *betimes* quickly **166** *nothing* no
one **169** *marked* noticed **170** *modern ecstasy* commonplace emotion **171**
for who for whom it tolls **173** *or ere* before; *relation* report **174** *nice* particular **175** *hiss* mock

176   Each minute teems a new one.

MACDUFF   How does my wife?

ROSS

    Why, well.

MACDUFF   And all my children?

ROSS   Well too.

MACDUFF

    The tyrant has not battered at their peace?

ROSS

    No, they were well at peace when I did leave 'em.

MACDUFF

180   Be not a niggard of your speech. How goes't?

ROSS

    When I came hither to transport the tidings
182   Which I have heavily borne, there ran a rumor
183   Of many worthy fellows that were out,
184   Which was to my belief witnessed the rather
    For that I saw the tyrant's power afoot.
    Now is the time of help. Your eye in Scotland
    Would create soldiers, make our women fight
    To doff their dire distresses.

MALCOLM   Be't their comfort

    We are coming thither. Gracious England hath
190   Lent us good Siward and ten thousand men,
    An older and a better soldier none
    That Christendom gives out.

ROSS   Would I could answer

    This comfort with the like. But I have words
    That would be howled out in the desert air,
195   Where hearing should not latch them.

MACDUFF   What concern they,

---

176 *teems* brings forth   182 *heavily borne* sadly brought   183 *out* in arms
184–85 *Which . . . afoot* i.e., the fact that I saw Macbeth's troops on the
march confirms my belief that his enemies, too, are mobilized   195 *latch*
catch

The general cause or is it a fee-grief   196
Due to some single breast?

ROSS   No mind that's honest
But in it shares some woe, though the main part
Pertains to you alone.

MACDUFF   If it be mine,
Keep it not from me; quickly let me have it.   *200*

ROSS
Let not your ears despise my tongue forever,
Which shall possess them with the heaviest sound
That ever yet they heard.

MACDUFF   Hmm – I guess at it.

ROSS
Your castle is surprised, your wife and babes
Savagely slaughtered. To relate the manner
Were, on the quarry of these murdered deer,   206
To add the death of you.

MALCOLM   Merciful heaven –
    [To Macduff]
What, man, ne'er pull your hat upon your brows.   208
Give sorrow words. The grief that does not speak   209
Whispers the o'erfraught heart and bids it break.   210

MACDUFF
My children too?

ROSS   Wife, children, servants, all
That could be found.   212

MACDUFF   And I must be from thence?
My wife killed too?

ROSS   I have said.

MALCOLM   Be comforted.
Let's make us med'cines of our great revenge

196–97 *fee-grief/Due* private grief belonging (from "fee simple," absolute
legal possession) **206** *quarry* heap of game **208** *upon your brows* down
over your eyes **209** *speak* i.e., speak to other people **210** *Whispers* whispers to **212** *from thence* away from home

To cure this deadly grief.

MACDUFF
He has no children. All my pretty ones?
Did you say all? O hellkite! All?
What, all my pretty chickens and their dam

219   At one fell swoop?

MALCOLM

220   Dispute it like a man.

MACDUFF   I shall do so;
But I must also feel it as a man.
I cannot but remember such things were
That were most precious to me. Did heaven look on
And would not take their part? Sinful Macduff,

225   They were all struck for thee. Naught that I am,
Not for their own demerits but for mine
Fell slaughter on their souls. Heaven rest them now.

MALCOLM
Be this the whetstone of your sword. Let grief
Convert to anger; blunt not the heart, enrage it.

MACDUFF

230   O, I could play the woman with mine eyes
And braggart with my tongue. But, gentle heavens,

232   Cut short all intermission. Front to front
Bring thou this fiend of Scotland and myself.
Within my sword's length set him. If he scape,
Heaven forgive him too.

MALCOLM   This tune goes manly.

236   Come, go we to the king. Our power is ready;

237   Our lack is nothing but our leave. Macbeth
Is ripe for shaking, and the pow'rs above

239   Put on their instruments. Receive what cheer you may.

240   The night is long that never finds the day.   *Exeunt.*

---

219 *fell* savage   220 *Dispute* confront, contend with   225 *Naught* wicked
230 *play . . . eyes* weep   232 *intermission* interval; *Front to front* face to face
236 *power* army   237 *Our . . . leave* we lack only formal permission to de-
part   239 *Put . . . instruments* urge on their agents

*

∾ **V.1** *Enter a Doctor of Physic and a Waiting Gentlewoman.*

DOCTOR   I have two nights watched with you, but can
perceive no truth in your report. When was it she last
walked?

GENTLEWOMAN   Since his majesty went into the field I
have seen her rise from her bed, throw her nightgown   5
upon her, unlock her closet, take forth paper, fold it,   6
write upon't, read it, afterwards seal it, and again return
to bed; yet all this while in a most fast sleep.

DOCTOR   A great perturbation in nature, to receive at
once the benefit of sleep and do the effects of watching.   10
In this slumb'ry agitation, besides her walking and
other actual performances, what at any time have you
heard her say?

GENTLEWOMAN   That, sir, which I will not report after
her.

DOCTOR   You may to me, and 'tis most meet you should.   16

GENTLEWOMAN   Neither to you nor anyone, having no   17
witness to confirm my speech.
        Enter Lady [Macbeth], with a taper.
Lo you, here she comes. This is her very guise, and,   19
upon my life, fast asleep. Observe her; stand close.   20

DOCTOR   How came she by that light?

GENTLEWOMAN   Why, it stood by her. She has light by
her continually. 'Tis her command.

DOCTOR   You see her eyes are open.

V.1 Macbeth's castle at Dunsinane   **5** *nightgown* dressing gown   **6** *closet*
chest or cabinet   **10** *do . . . watching* act as if awake   **16** *meet* fitting
17–18 *having . . . speech* (the gentlewoman's report would amount to charg-
ing the king with murder, which would be treasonable)   **19** *guise* custom
20 *close* concealed

GENTLEWOMAN   Ay, but their sense are shut.

DOCTOR   What is it she does now? Look how she rubs
her hands.

GENTLEWOMAN   It is an accustomed action with her, to
seem thus washing her hands. I have known her con-
30   tinue in this a quarter of an hour.

LADY MACBETH   Yet here's a spot.

DOCTOR   Hark, she speaks. I will set down what comes
from her, to satisfy my remembrance the more
strongly.

LADY MACBETH   Out, damned spot! Out, I say! One –
two – why then 'tis time to do't. Hell is murky. Fie, my
lord, fie! a soldier and afeard? What need we fear who
knows it, when none can call our power to account? Yet
who would have thought the old man to have had so
40   much blood in him?

DOCTOR   Do you mark that?

42   LADY MACBETH   The Thane of Fife had a wife. Where is
she now? What, will these hands ne'er be clean? No
more o' that, my lord, no more o' that. You mar all with
45   this starting.

46   DOCTOR   Go to, go to! You have known what you
should not.

GENTLEWOMAN   She has spoke what she should not, I
am sure of that. Heaven knows what she has known.

50   LADY MACBETH   Here's the smell of the blood still. All
the perfumes of Arabia will not sweeten this little hand.
Oh, oh, oh!

53   DOCTOR   What a sigh is there. The heart is sorely charged.

GENTLEWOMAN   I would not have such a heart in my
55   bosom for the dignity of the whole body.

DOCTOR   Well, well, well.

GENTLEWOMAN   Pray God it be, sir.

---

42 *Thane of Fife* Macduff   45 *starting* flinching   46 *Go to, go to* come, come
53 *sorely charged* heavily burdened   55 *dignity* high rank (i.e., as queen)

DOCTOR   This disease is beyond my practice. Yet I have 58
    known those which have walked in their sleep who
    have died holily in their beds. 60
LADY MACBETH   Wash your hands, put on your night-
    gown, look not so pale. I tell you yet again, Banquo's
    buried. He cannot come out on's grave.
DOCTOR   Even so?
LADY MACBETH   To bed, to bed; there's knocking at the
    gate. Come, come, come, come, give me your hand.
    What's done cannot be undone. To bed, to bed, to bed.
                                            Exit.

DOCTOR   Will she go now to bed?
GENTLEWOMAN   Directly.
DOCTOR
    Foul whisp'rings are abroad. Unnatural deeds 70
    Do breed unnatural troubles. Infected minds
    To their deaf pillows will discharge their secrets.
    More needs she the divine than the physician.
    God, God forgive us all. Look after her;
    Remove from her the means of all annoyance, 75
    And still keep eyes upon her. So good night.
    My mind she has mated, and amazed my sight. 77
    I think, but dare not speak.
GENTLEWOMAN   Good night, good doctor.
                                            Exeunt.

                    *

∾ **V.2** *Drum and Colors. Enter Menteith, Caithness,*
    Angus, Lennox, Soldiers.

MENTEITH
    The English pow'r is near, led on by Malcolm,

---

58 *practice* professional skill 75 *annoyance* harm, trouble 77 *mated* de-
feated (cf. checkmate)
    V.2 Open country near Dunsinane **s.d.** *Drum and Colors* drummers and
standard-bearers

His uncle Siward, and the good Macduff.
3   Revenges burn in them; for their dear causes
4   Would to the bleeding and the grim alarm
5   Excite the mortified man.

ANGUS   Near Birnam Wood
Shall we well meet them; that way are they coming.

CAITHNESS
Who knows if Donalbain be with his brother?

LENNOX
8   For certain, sir, he is not. I have a file
Of all the gentry. There is Siward's son
10   And many unrough youths that even now
11   Protest their first of manhood.

MENTEITH   What does the tyrant?

CAITHNESS
Great Dunsinane he strongly fortifies.
Some say he's mad; others that lesser hate him
Do call it valiant fury; but for certain
15   He cannot buckle his distempered cause
16   Within the belt of rule.

ANGUS   Now does he feel
His secret murders sticking on his hands.
18   Now minutely revolts upbraid his faith breach.
19   Those he commands move only in command,
20   Nothing in love. Now does he feel his title
Hang loose about him, like a giant's robe
Upon a dwarfish thief.

MENTEITH   Who then shall blame
23   His pestered senses to recoil and start,
When all that is within him does condemn
Itself for being there?

─────────

3 *Revenges burn* desire for revenge burns   4 *bleeding* shedding of blood   5
Excite incite; *mortified* dead   8 *file* list   10 *unrough* beardless   11 *Protest* as-
sert   15 *distempered* diseased   16 *rule* authority   18 *minutely* every minute;
revolts rebellions; *faith breach* broken faith   19 *in command* under orders
23 *pestered* tormented

CAITHNESS   Well, march we on
   To give obedience where 'tis truly owed.
   Meet we the med'cine of the sickly weal;   27
   And with him pour we in our country's purge
   Each drop of us.
LENNOX   Or so much as it needs
   To dew the sovereign flower and drown the weeds.   30
   Make we our march towards Birnam.
                       Exeunt, marching.

＊

⌘ **V.3** *Enter Macbeth, Doctor, and Attendants.*

MACBETH
   Bring me no more reports. Let them fly all.
   Till Birnam Wood remove to Dunsinane,
   I cannot taint with fear. What's the boy Malcolm?   3
   Was he not born of woman? The spirits that know
   All mortal consequences have pronounced me thus: 5
   "Fear not, Macbeth. No man that's born of woman
   Shall e'er have power upon thee." Then fly, false thanes,
   And mingle with the English epicures.   8
   The mind I sway by and the heart I bear   9
   Shall never sag with doubt nor shake with fear.   10
     Enter Servant.
   The devil damn thee black, thou cream-faced loon!   11
   Where got'st thou that goose look?   12
SERVANT
   There is ten thousand –
MACBETH   Geese, villain?
SERVANT   Soldiers, sir.

---

27 *med'cine* physician (i.e., Malcolm); *weal* state 30 *dew* water
   V.3 Within Macbeth's castle at Dunsinane 3 *taint* grow weak 5 *mortal consequences* human eventualities 8 *English epicures* pleasure-loving English
9 *I sway by* (1) that rules me, (2) that I rule by 11 *cream-faced* pale (with fear); *loon* scoundrel 12 *goose* foolish

MACBETH

16   Go prick thy face and over-red thy fear,
17   Thou lily-livered boy. What soldiers, patch?
      Death of thy soul! those linen cheeks of thine
      Are counselors to fear. What soldiers, whey-face?

SERVANT

20   The English force, so please you.

MACBETH

      Take thy face hence.   *[Exit Servant.]*
                   Seyton! – I am sick at heart,
22   When I behold – Seyton, I say! – This push
23   Will cheer me ever, or disseat me now.
      I have lived long enough. My way of life
25   Is fall'n into the sere, the yellow leaf,
      And that which should accompany old age,
      As honor, love, obedience, troops of friends,
      I must not look to have; but, in their stead,
      Curses not loud but deep, mouth-honor, breath,
30   Which the poor heart would fain deny, and dare not.
      Seyton!
           Enter Seyton.

SEYTON

      What's your gracious pleasure?

MACBETH   What news more?

SEYTON

      All is confirmed, my lord, which was reported.

MACBETH

      I'll fight till from my bones my flesh be hacked.
      Give me my armor.

SEYTON   'Tis not needed yet.

MACBETH

      I'll put it on.

37   Send out more horses, skirr the country round,

---

16 *over-red* paint red (i.e., with ruddy courage)   17 *patch* fool   22 *push* attack   23 *disseat* unseat   25 *sere* dry, withered   37 *horses* horsemen; *skirr* scour

Hang those that talk of fear. Give me mine armor.
How does your patient, doctor?
DOCTOR   Not so sick, my lord,
As she is troubled with thick-coming fancies   40
That keep her from her rest.
MACBETH   Cure her of that.
Canst thou not minister to a mind diseased,
Pluck from the memory a rooted sorrow,
Raze out the written troubles of the brain,   44
And with some sweet oblivious antidote   45
Cleanse the stuffed bosom of that perilous stuff
Which weighs upon the heart?
DOCTOR   Therein the patient
Must minister to himself.
MACBETH
Throw physic to the dogs, I'll none of it.   49
    [To an Attendant]
Come, put mine armor on. Give me my staff.   50
Seyton, send out. – Doctor, the thanes fly from me. –
Come, sir, dispatch. – If thou couldst, doctor, cast   52
The water of my land, find her disease,
And purge it to a sound and pristine health,
I would applaud thee to the very echo,
That should applaud again. – Pull't off, I say. –
What rhubarb, senna, or what purgative drug
Would scour these English hence? Hear'st thou of them?
DOCTOR
Ay, my good lord. Your royal preparation
Makes us hear something.   60
MACBETH   Bring it after me.
I will not be afraid of death and bane   61
Till Birnam Forest come to Dunsinane.
                          Exeunt [all but the Doctor].

---

44 *Raze out* erase   **45** *oblivious* causing forgetfulness   **49** *physic* medicine
52 *dispatch* hurry   **52–53** *cast . . . water* analyze the urine (as a way of diag-
nosing illness)   **60** *it* i.e., the remaining armor   **61** *bane* destruction

DOCTOR
 Were I from Dunsinane away and clear,
 Profit again should hardly draw me here.   *[Exit.]*

                            *

❧ **V.4** *Drum and Colors. Enter Malcolm, Siward, Mac-*
 duff, Siward's Son, Menteith, Caithness, Angus,
 [Lennox, Ross,] and Soldiers, marching.

MALCOLM
 Cousins, I hope the days are near at hand
2 That chambers will be safe.
MENTEITH   We doubt it nothing.
SIWARD
 What wood is this before us?
MENTEITH   The Wood of Birnam.
MALCOLM
 Let every soldier hew him down a bough
5 And bear't before him. Thereby shall we shadow
6 The numbers of our host and make discovery
 Err in report of us.
SOLDIER   It shall be done.
SIWARD
 We learn no other but the confident tyrant
 Keeps still in Dunsinane and will endure
10 Our setting down before't.
MALCOLM   'Tis his main hope,
11 For where there is advantage to be given
12 Both more and less have given him the revolt,
 And none serve with him but constrainèd things
14 Whose hearts are absent too.
MACDUFF   Let our just censures

V.4 Before Birnam Wood **2** *chambers* private rooms (i.e., our homes); *noth-*
ing not at all **5** *shadow* conceal **6** *discovery* (Macbeth's) reconnaissance **10**
setting down before laying siege to **11** *where . . . given* as the opportunity
presents itself **12** *more . . . revolt* high and low (i.e., nobility and common-
ers) have rebelled against him **14** *just censures* impartial judgment

Attend the true event, and put we on   15
Industrious soldiership.
SIWARD   The time approaches
That will with due decision make us know
What we shall say we have and what we owe.
Thoughts speculative their unsure hopes relate,
But certain issue strokes must arbitrate –   20
Towards which advance the war.   *Exeunt, marching.*   21

*

∾ **V.5** *Enter Macbeth, Seyton, and Soldiers, with Drum and Colors.*

MACBETH
Hang out our banners on the outward walls.
The cry is still, "They come." Our castle's strength
Will laugh a siege to scorn. Here let them lie
Till famine and the ague eat them up.   4
Were they not forced with those that should be ours,   5
We might have met them dareful, beard to beard,   6
And beat them backward home.
    A cry within of women.   What is that noise?
SEYTON
It is the cry of women, my good lord.   *[Exit.]*
MACBETH
I have almost forgot the taste of fears.
The time has been my senses would have cooled   *10*
To hear a night-shriek, and my fell of hair   *11*
Would at a dismal treatise rouse and stir   *12*
As life were in't. I have supped full with horrors.
Direness, familiar to my slaughterous thoughts,   *14*
Cannot once start me.   *15*

---

15 *Attend . . . event* await the actual result 20 *certain . . . arbitrate* blows must decide the final outcome 21 *war* army
    V.5 Inside Macbeth's castle 4 *ague* fever 5 *forced* reinforced 6 *dareful* defiant 11 *fell* head 12 *dismal treatise* frightening story 14 *Direness* horror 15 *start* frighten

[Enter Seyton.]   Wherefore was that cry?

SEYTON

    The queen, my lord, is dead.

MACBETH

    She should have died hereafter:

18   There would have been a time for such a word.

    Tomorrow, and tomorrow, and tomorrow

20   Creeps in this petty pace from day to day

    To the last syllable of recorded time,

    And all our yesterdays have lighted fools

    The way to dusty death. Out, out, brief candle,

    Life's but a walking shadow, a poor player

    That struts and frets his hour upon the stage

    And then is heard no more. It is a tale

    Told by an idiot, full of sound and fury,

    Signifying nothing.

       Enter a Messenger.

    Thou com'st to use thy tongue: thy story quickly.

MESSENGER

30   Gracious my lord,

31   I should report that which I say I saw,

    But know not how to do't.

MACBETH   Well, say, sir.

MESSENGER

    As I did stand my watch upon the hill,

    I looked toward Birnam, and anon methought

    The wood began to move.

MACBETH   Liar and slave!

MESSENGER

    Let me endure your wrath if't be not so.

    Within this three mile may you see it coming.

    I say, a moving grove.

MACBETH   If thou speak'st false,

    Upon the next tree shalt thou hang alive

40   Till famine cling thee. If thy speech be sooth,

---

18 *a time* i.e., an appropriate time   31 *say* insist   40 *cling* shrivel; *sooth* truth

I care not if thou dost for me as much.
I pull in resolution, and begin   42
To doubt th' equivocation of the fiend   43
That lies like truth. "Fear not, till Birnam Wood
Do come to Dunsinane," and now a wood
Comes toward Dunsinane. Arm, arm, and out!
If this which he avouches does appear,   47
There is nor flying hence nor tarrying here.
I 'gin to be aweary of the sun,
And wish th' estate o' th' world were now undone.   50
Ring the alarum bell! Blow wind, come wrack,
At least we'll die with harness on our back.   *Exeunt.*   52

                              *

⁊ **V.6** *Drum and Colors. Enter Malcolm, Siward, Mac-*
    duff, and their Army, with boughs.

MALCOLM
  Now near enough. Your leafy screens throw down
  And show like those you are. You, worthy uncle,
  Shall with my cousin, your right noble son,
  Lead our first battle. Worthy Macduff and we   4
  Shall take upon's what else remains to do,
  According to our order.   6
SIWARD   Fare you well.
  Do we but find the tyrant's power tonight,   7
  Let us be beaten if we cannot fight.
MACDUFF
  Make all our trumpets speak, give them all breath,
  Those clamorous harbingers of blood and death.   10
                        Exeunt. Alarums continued.
                              *

---

42 *pull in* curb, check   43 *doubt* suspect; *equivocation* double-talk   47
avouches affirms   50 *estate* order   52 *harness* armor
  V.6 Fields outside Dunsinane Castle   4 *battle* battalion   6 *order* battle
plan   7 *power* forces

∾ **V.7** *Enter Macbeth.*

MACBETH
They have tied me to a stake. I cannot fly,
2   But bearlike I must fight the course. What's he
That was not born of woman? Such a one
Am I to fear, or none.
          Enter Young Siward.
YOUNG SIWARD
What is thy name?
MACBETH   Thou'lt be afraid to hear it.
YOUNG SIWARD
No, though thou call'st thyself a hotter name
Than any is in hell.
MACBETH   My name's Macbeth.
YOUNG SIWARD
The devil himself could not pronounce a title
More hateful to mine ear.
MACBETH   No, nor more fearful.
YOUNG SIWARD
10   Thou liest, abhorrèd tyrant! With my sword
I'll prove the lie thou speak'st.
          Fight, and Young Siward slain.
MACBETH   Thou wast born of woman.
But swords I smile at, weapons laugh to scorn,
Brandished by man that's of a woman born.
                         Exit [with Young Siward's body].
          Alarums. Enter Macduff.
MACDUFF
That way the noise is. Tyrant, show thy face!
If thou beest slain and with no stroke of mine,
My wife and children's ghosts will haunt me still.
17   I cannot strike at wretched kerns, whose arms
18   Are hired to bear their staves. Either thou, Macbeth,

V.7 The same   **2** *course* attack (like a bear tied to a stake and baited by dogs)
17 *kerns* mercenary foot soldiers   **18** *staves* lances

Or else my sword with an unbattered edge
I sheathe again undeeded. There thou shouldst be –   20
By this great clatter one of greatest note   21
Seems bruited. Let me find him, Fortune,   22
And more I beg not.   *Exit. Alarums.*
 Enter Malcolm and Siward.

SIWARD
This way, my lord. The castle's gently rendered: 24
The tyrant's people on both sides do fight,
The noble thanes do bravely in the war,
The day almost itself professes yours   27
And little is to do.

MALCOLM   We have met with foes
That strike beside us.   29

SIWARD   Enter, sir, the castle.
            Exeunt. Alarum.

         *

∾ **V.8** *Enter Macbeth.*

MACBETH
Why should I play the Roman fool and die
On mine own sword? Whiles I see lives, the gashes   2
Do better upon them.
 Enter Macduff.

MACDUFF   Turn, hellhound, turn!

MACBETH
Of all men else I have avoided thee.
But get thee back. My soul is too much charged   5
With blood of thine already.

MACDUFF   I have no words;
My voice is in my sword, thou bloodier villain

---

20 *undeeded* having done nothing 21 *note* importance 22 *bruited* indicated,
noised 24 *gently rendered* surrendered calmly (or nobly) 27 *itself professes* de-
clares itself 29 *strike beside us* (1) fight on our side, (2) strike to one side of us
 V.8 2 *Whiles . . . lives* as long as I see living creatures 5 *charged* burdened

8   Than terms can give thee out.
      Fight. Alarum.

MACBETH   Thou losest labor.
9   As easy mayst thou the intrenchant air
10   With thy keen sword impress as make me bleed.
     Let fall thy blade on vulnerable crests.
     I bear a charmèd life, which must not yield
13   To one of woman born.

MACDUFF   Despair thy charm,
14   And let the angel whom thou still hast served
     Tell thee, Macduff was from his mother's womb
     Untimely ripped.

MACBETH
     Accursèd be that tongue that tells me so,
18   For it hath cowed my better part of man;
19   And be these juggling fiends no more believed,
20   That palter with us in a double sense,
     That keep the word of promise to our ear
     And break it to our hope. I'll not fight with thee.

MACDUFF
23   Then yield thee coward,
     And live to be the show and gaze o' th' time.
25   We'll have thee, as our rarer monsters are,
26   Painted upon a pole, and underwrit
     "Here may you see the tyrant."

MACBETH   I will not yield,
     To kiss the ground before young Malcolm's feet
     And to be baited with the rabble's curse.
30   Though Birnam Wood be come to Dunsinane,
     And thou opposed, being of no woman born,
     Yet I will try the last. Before my body

---

8 *give thee out* describe you   9 *intrenchant* incapable of being cut   10 *impress* mark   13 *charm* magic   14 *angel* guardian spirit; *still* always   18 *cowed* made cowardly; *better . . . man* most of what makes me a man   19 *juggling* deceiving, quibbling   20 *palter with us* equivocate to us, trick us   23 *yield thee coward* surrender as, or concede that you are, a coward   25 *monsters* freaks   26 *Painted . . . pole* depicted on a signboard

I throw my warlike shield. Lay on, Macduff,
And damned be him that first cries "Hold, enough!"
Exeunt fighting. Alarums. [Re]enter fighting, and
Macbeth slain. [Exit Macduff with Macbeth's body.]

Retreat and flourish. Enter, with Drum and Colors,
Malcolm, Siward, Ross, Thanes, and Soldiers.

MALCOLM
I would the friends we miss were safe arrived.

SIWARD
Some must go off; and yet, by these I see,   36
So great a day as this is cheaply bought.

MALCOLM
Macduff is missing, and your noble son.

ROSS
Your son, my lord, has paid a soldier's debt.
He only lived but till he was a man,   40
The which no sooner had his prowess confirmed
In the unshrinking station where he fought   42
But like a man he died.

SIWARD   Then he is dead?

ROSS
Ay, and brought off the field. Your cause of sorrow
Must not be measured by his worth, for then
It hath no end.   46

SIWARD   Had he his hurts before?

ROSS
Ay, on the front.

SIWARD   Why then, God's soldier be he.
Had I as many sons as I have hairs,
I would not wish them to a fairer death:
And so his knell is knolled.   50

MALCOLM   He's worth more sorrow,

---

36 *go off* perish; *these* i.e., these here assembled   **42** *unshrinking station* place
from which he did not retreat   **46** *Had ... before* were his wounds on the
front of his body (i.e., was he running away)   **50** *knolled* tolled

And that I'll spend for him.

SIWARD   He's worth no more.
52   They say he parted well and paid his score,
     And so, God be with him. Here comes newer comfort.
         Enter Macduff, with Macbeth's head.

MACDUFF
     Hail, king, for so thou art. Behold where stands
     Th' usurper's cursèd head. The time is free.
56   I see thee compassed with thy kingdom's pearl,
     That speak my salutation in their minds,
     Whose voices I desire aloud with mine –
     Hail, King of Scotland!

ALL   Hail, King of Scotland!
         Flourish.

MALCOLM
60   We shall not spend a large expense of time
61   Before we reckon with your several loves
62   And make us even with you. My thanes and kinsmen,
     Henceforth be earls, the first that ever Scotland
     In such an honor named. What's more to do
65   Which would be planted newly with the time –
     As calling home our exiled friends abroad
     That fled the snares of watchful tyranny,
68   Producing forth the cruel ministers
     Of this dead butcher and his fiendlike queen,
70   Who, as 'tis thought, by self and violent hands
     Took off her life – this, and what needful else
     That calls upon us, by the grace of Grace
73   We will perform in measure, time, and place.
     So thanks to all at once and to each one,
     Whom we invite to see us crowned at Scone.
                              Flourish. Exeunt omnes.

---

52 *score* reckoning   56 *compassed* surrounded; *kingdom's pearl* what is most valuable in the kingdom (i.e., the assembled nobility)   61 *reckon* settle accounts   62 *make . . . with* repay our debts to   65 *planted . . . time* done at the beginning of the new era   68 *ministers* agents   70 *self and violent* her own violent   73 *perform in measure, time* duly perform at the appropriate time